SHIP MODELS IN MINIATURE

SHIP MODELS IN MINIATURE

Donald McNarry

With photographs by the author

PRAEGER PUBLISHERS
New York

By the same author
SHIPBUILDING IN MINIATURE

Published in the United States of America in 1975
by Praeger Publishers, Inc.
111 Fourth Avenue, New York, N.Y. 10003

Library of Congress Card Catalog Number: 74-32599

ISBN: 0-275-22490-2

Printed in Great Britain

CONTENTS

Page 6   List of Models

8   List of Colour Plates

9   Introduction

16   1. The 'Too-Early' Models

24   2. The Seventeenth Century

72   3. The Eighteenth Century

88   4. The Nineteenth Century

158   5. The Twentieth Century

175   Glossary

LIST OF MODELS

The 'Too-Early' Models

1. A Phoenician Galley (c700 BC) scale 32′–1″ 3″ long
2. A Flemish Carrack (c1480) scale 16′–1″ 8½″ long
3. A Portuguese Caravel (c1500) scale 32′–1″ 3⅜″ long
4. *Elizabeth Jonas* (c1598) Elizabethan galleon scale 32′–1″ 7½″ long

The Seventeenth Century

5. *Prince Royal* (1610) 50/60-gun, 3-decker scale 32′–1″ 7½″ long
6. *Haerlem* (c1640) Dutch East Indiaman scale 32′–1″ 5¾″ long
7. *Dromedaris* (c1652) Dutch pinasschip scale 16′–1″ 7¼″ long
8. *Naseby* (1655) 80-gun, 3-decker scale 16′–1″ 12⅝″ long
9. HMY *Mary* (1660) 8-gun, royal yacht scale 16′–1″ 6¼″ long
10. HMS *Royal Escape* (1660) 4-gun smack scale 16′–1″ 4″ long
11. Royal Yachts (seventeenth century) scales 16′, 32′ & 64′–1″, 7″, 3½″ & 1¾″ long
12. HMS *Royal Charles* (c1666) 80-gun, 3-decker scale 64′–1″ 3⅝″ long
13. HMS *Resolution* (1667) 70-gun, 3rd rate, 2-decker scale 16′–1″ 11½″ long
14. HMS *Prince* (1670) 100-gun, 1st rate, 3-decker scale 32′–1″ 6⅜″ long
15. HMY *Kitchen* (1670) 6-gun, royal yacht scale 16′–1″ 5¼″ long
16. HMS *James Galley* (1676) 30-gun, galley frigate scale 32′–1″ 4⅞″ long
17. HMS *Grafton* (1679) 70-gun, 3rd rate, 2-decker scale 16′–1″ 13⅝″ long
18. HMS *Tiger* (1681) 46-gun, 4th rate, 2-decker scale 16′–1″ 9⅜″ long
19. HMS *Britannia* (1682) 100-gun, 1st rate, 3-decker scale 16′–1″ 13⅛ & 15¼″ long
20. HMS *St Albans* (1687) 50-gun, 4th rate, 2-decker scales 16′ & 32′–1″ 9½″ & 5⅞″ long
21. HMS *Lizard* (1697) 24-gun, 6th rate, single decker scale 16′–1″ 7⅛″ long

The Eighteenth Century

22. *Mediator* (1742) Colonial American sloop scale 16′–1″ 8¾″ long
23. HMS *Medway* (1742) 60-gun, 4th rate, 2-decker scale 16′–1″ 14¾″ long
24. *Grosvenor* (1770) 26-gun East Indiaman scale 16′–1″ 13¾″ long
25. HMS *Queen Charlotte* (1790) 100-gun, 1st rate, 3-decker scale 32′–1″ 9¾″ long
26. HMS *Brunswick* (1790) 74-gun, 2-decker scale 16′–1″ 13⅛″ long
27. *Constitution* (c1798) US frigate scale 16′–1″ 18½″ long

The Nineteenth Century

28. HMS *Euryalus* (c1805) 36-gun frigate scale 32′–1″ 8″ long
29. HMS *Victory* (c1805) 100-gun, 3-decker scale 32′–1″ 10⅜″ long
30. *Hecate* (c1818) 18-gun brig-of-war scale 16′–1″ 11¾″ long
31. *Great Western* (1837) Paddle steamer scale 32′–1″ 8½″ long
32. *Archimedes* (1838) Screw steamer scale 16′–1″ 11¼″ long

33. HMS *Southampton* (c1840)   52-gun, 4th rate   scale 32′–1″   10″ long
34. *Britannia* (1840)   Cunard paddle steamer   scale 50′–1″   5⅞″ long
35. *Great Britain* (1843)   Screw steamer   scale 32′–1″   10½″ long
36. *Staghound* (1850)   US clipper   scale 32′–1″   10″ long
37. *Nightingale* (1851)   US clipper   scale 32′–1″   8¾″ long
38. *Witch of the Wave* (1851)   US clipper   scale 32′–1″   9¼″ long
39. *Challenge* (1851)   US clipper   scale 32′–1″   11″ long
40. *Flying Fish* (1851)   US clipper   scale 32′–1″   9¼″ long
41. *Flying Cloud* (1851)   US clipper   scale 16′–1″   18½″ long
42. *Sovereign of the Seas* (1852)   US clipper   scale 32′–1″   9¾″ long
43. *Sweepstakes* (1853)   US clipper   scale 32′–1″   10¾″ long
44. *Great Republic* (1853)   US clipper   scale 32′–1″   13¾″ long
45. *Lightning* (1854)   US clipper   scale 16′–1″   20¾″ long
46. HMS *Birkenhead* (1852)   Paddle troopship   scale 32′–1″   9¼″ long
47. *Scotia* (1861)   Cunard paddle steamer   scale 50′–1″   8¾″ long
48. CSS *Alabama* (1862)   Confederate States raider   scale 32′–1″   8¾″ long
49. *Great Eastern* (c1865)   Screw/paddle steamer   scale 32′–1″   22″ long
50. *Taeping* (1863)   Clipper   scales 32′ & 64′–1″   8½″ & 4¼″ long
51. *Ariel* (1865)   Clipper   scales 32′ & 64′–1″   8½″ & 4¼″ long
52. *Sir Lancelot* (1865)   Clipper   scales 16′ & 32′–1″   17″ & 8½″ long
53. *Carnarvon Castle* (1867)   Clipper   scales 32′ & 50′–1″   9⅛″ & 6″ long
54. *Thermopylae* (1868)   Clipper   scale 32′–1″   9″ long
55. *Cutty Sark* (1869)   Clipper   scale 32′–1″   9⅛″ long
56. *Servia* (1881)   Cunard liner   scale 50′–1″   10¾″ long
57. USS *Oregon* (1895)   US warship   scale 32′–1″   11″ long

The Twentieth Century

58. *Herzogin Cecilie* (1902)   Four-masted barque   scale 32′–1″   11⅝″ long
59. *Armadale Castle* (1903)   Union Castle liner   scale 32′–1″   18¾″ long
60. *Waratah* (1908)   Blue Anchor liner   scale 32′–1″   15¾″ long
61. HM Warships (c. World War II)   scale 100′–1″   6¾″, 3½″, 3½″ & 2¾″ long
62. *Rhodesia Castle* (1951)   Union Castle liner   scale 16′–1″   36″ long
63. HMY *Britannia* (1953)   Royal yacht   scale 32′–1″   13″ long
64. *Sir Winston Churchill* (c1969)   Training schooner   scale 16′–1″   10¼″ long
65. *Bloodhound* (c1969)   Royal racing yacht   scale 6′–1″   10½″ long

LIST OF COLOUR PLATES

Haerlem   scale 32′–1″   5¾″ long   (see p. 33)

Naseby   scale 16′–1″   12⅝″ long   (see p. 33)

Prince Royal   scale 32′–1″   7½″ long   (see p. 34)

HMY *Kitchen*   scale 16′–1″   5¼″ long (see p. 35)

HMS *Britannia*   scale 16′–1″   13⅛″ long   (see p. 35)

HMS *Queen Charlotte*   scale 32′–1″   9¾″ long   (see p. 36)

Constitution   scale 16′–1″   18½″ long (see p. 36)

HMS *Resolution*   scale 16′–1″   11½″ long (see p. 37)

HMS *Medway*   scale 16′–1″   14¾″ long   (see p. 38)

HMS *Brunswick*   scale 16′–1″   13⅛″ long   (see p. 39)

HMY *Mary*   scale 16′–1″   6¼″ long (see p. 40)

Nightingale   scale 32′–1″   8⅜″ long   (see p. 105)

Sweepstakes   scale 32′–1″   10¾″ long   (see p. 106)

HMS *Southampton*   scale 32′–1″   10″ long (see p. 107)

Sir Winston Churchill   scale 16′–1″   10¼″ long   (see p. 108)

Great Republic   scale 32′–1″   13¾″ long   (see p. 109)

Servia   scale 50′–1″   10¾″ long   (see p. 110)

Armadale Castle   scale 32′–1″   18⅜″ long   (see p. 111)

HMY *Britannia*   scale 32′–1″   13″ long   (see p. 111)

Archimedes   scale 16′–1″   11¼″ long   (see p. 112)

INTRODUCTION

In my previous book *Shipbuilding in Miniature* published by the late Percival Marshall & Co, London, in 1955 and long since out of print, I described the building of some of the models I made as a spare-time ship modeller between 1946 and 1953. It was written when I was changing from amateur to free-lance professional. This book is also written with a change in the wind, when in order to avoid the difficulties of a new English sales tax I can no longer undertake specific commissions but have to reverse the whole process and offer what I make to interested clients.

The Scope The following pages describe a selection of the models built during the last twenty years. The historical period covered is from 700 BC to the late 1960s, the types of models: scenic, waterline, full hull and Admiralty Board dockyard models, and the scales – with one exception – reasonably miniature: 100'–1" to 16'–1". This time the emphasis is more on the description of the models and the data sources from which they were made rather than on the methods of construction.

Professional Ship Model Building I believe no one before has written anything from the purely professional economic point of view of the self-employed, free-lance ship model builder. Judging from the various enquiries I get from young hopefuls, and oblique questions from others, perhaps these details of such an unusual occupation might be of interest.

The Required Attitude First of all one has to subscribe whole-heartedly to some sound, old-fashioned and out-of-date principles: that the quality of the product comes first, that hard work and discipline are good for their own sake, and that some modern ideas to the contrary are wrong.

The Time Factor This is the most important aspect of the whole business. Detailed miniature ship models take a long, long time to construct; time which cannot be reduced under any circumstances if by so doing the quality of work is impaired, but which can be reduced by increasing experience, improved methods and materials and the occasional extra good idea. (If only one had all one's good ideas at the outset!)

Ship models are useless things and their only virtue lies in the accuracy and realism with which they depict the prototype in such a way as to give lasting pleasure to the beholder. Every ship model consists of hundreds, indeed thousands, of separate little pieces and to achieve the required effect every piece has to be made to the best of one's ability, to the correct shape and size and to the required colour, texture and finish, and it is making all these pieces that eats up the hours. The final assembly, although requiring forethought and a precise sequence is a mere flick of the wrist by comparison.

It will be seen from the above that the great charge on a model's price is the cost of the time, but against this there is the remarkable advantage that even in these days the cost of materials is almost negligible. A few pieces of firewood, some bits of metal and wire, the odd drop of paint and *enough time* will produce a £1000 ($2400) model.

The resulting further advantage of this, of course, is that the beginner needs very little initial capital, the tools and the materials of his would-be hobby, and enough money for his living expenses until he gets paid for his first model. At the beginning my wife and I just made it with one week's housekeeping to spare.

However, it really can be quite a leap in the dark, especially nowadays when society is more and more angled against the self-employed.

The Rate per Hour This is the great question everyone wishes to ask. How much is charged per hour? (It is curious that compatriots asking this seem impertinent while Americans do not!) When an amateur I remember writing to the late Mr Norman Ough and delicately skirting around the subject, and with professional commonsense he said that the work had to look worth £1 per hour and if it got a quarter of this one was lucky. This was twenty years ago and the principle is the same today.

However we can get nearer than this with an easy sum. On the basis of a meagre life-style, minimum weekly living expenses are accurately calculated. On a basis of optimistic stamina, maximum weekly working hours are accurately estimated. Simple division produces the result.

The Working Hours The trick is of course to maintain the maximum hours unvaryingly, week after week, year after year. This is not too difficult, the work is absorbing, the self-discipline required eases with application and the world outside becomes increasingly unpleasant.

Personally I find a regular routine, somewhat easier now than previously I must admit, produces the best work most expeditiously, 8 am to 1 pm and 2.30 to 7.30 pm, seven days a week, fifty-two weeks a year. Unfortunately one does have to sacrifice the odd day to research and correspondence and sadly I have yet to find a way of charging this to the customer!

Despite a regular system of work the problem of quoting a price beforehand is as far as I am concerned an insoluble one. In my experience it is certain that a variant of Parkinson's Law applies here: that the hours allotted for a model are always, and only, exceeded if a price has been quoted. It is a much better risk to refuse to quote a price and instead advise the client that he need not have the model if he finds it too expensive on completion. If he does then one still has the model, and its full value will be realised (in both senses of the word) eventually.

Creating Models The main reason for making ship models must be the satisfaction derived from converting, with moderate precision, rather pleasant and unusual materials – holly, box, ivory, copper, etc – into the completed miniature ship by means of a great variety of arts, crafts and processes. The work is in three dimensions, the tools are diverse, it is always different, it is always difficult and consequently never palls – so much more varied, engrossing and demanding surely than just painting a picture of a ship in two dimensions with one set of tools and one material, but not so profitable of course.

Rarely if ever is one satisfied with the result but the pleasure of doing it is worth the effort. I have never been in any doubt myself that this sheer enjoyment of the actual creation quite overrides all the general difficulties of making a living at a rather rarefied and specialized job in a world more and more given up to the mass production of the mediocre, and ever increasing official interference with the individual worker.

Collecting Models Why people buy and collect models is another matter altogether. The majority I feel sure do so because they think real, full-sized ships are beautiful objects and at the same time have a liking for small things which look delicate and complicated. It is interesting to note that the novice collector always wants an extreme example, the 120-gun ship or a clipper with more sails set than the wind could cope with!

Some make collections with a thematic interest. My models in the Cussons Collection in the Cape Town Castle Museum nearly all have historical South African connections. Another client has a most interesting and varied collection with all the cases of matching timber. Yet another customer has a representative collection of Cunarders all to the same scale, from the *Britannia* 1840 to the *Queen Elizabeth* of 1946; he also has Brunel's remarkable trio (the *Great Western*, the *Great Britain* and the *Great Eastern*).

The professional ship model builder is indeed fortunate if he has long-term clients such as these, as it is patronage of this sort that makes the whole thing possible.

One client, however, commenced what was going to be a unique collection (and my *magnum opus*) of Admiralty Board dockyard models of named examples of all the ship types in the seventeenth-century Royal Navy, but he, I fear, fell by the wayside.

Just occasionally I have thought that people want them because they are difficult to get, because they have to wait for them, because they cannot buy the same thing elsewhere and perhaps even because they are expensive.

Some collectors buy as an investment, and there is no doubt that models appreciate in value (a hint to the model builder not to sell all he makes perhaps) and in this respect it is absolutely essential that the glass covers of ship model cases should be firmly fitted down and something of a bother to remove. Providing they are left untouched and undamaged I see no reason why miniature ship models should not last almost indefinitely, and we hope give some pleasure and satisfaction to the collector's great grand-children. One of the reasons why so many of the Napoleonic models are so damaged is simply that the glass covers were easily removable.

Restoration Work This brings us to another aspect of professional ship modelling, that of restoration. As well as making my own models I have, over the years, restored well over sixty Napoleonic prisoner-of-war models, mostly miniatures.

As the reader may know these are much prized, highly thought of antiques in some demand and fetch high prices, but the fact is that the quality of the work on them is frequently pretty poor compared with the carefully made modern model.

In order to restore them a mental switch has to be made and all thoughts of accuracy, realism and immaculate finish are laid aside, concentration being rather on matching the existing. This is a much quicker and easier process than normal model building and consequently there is more money to be made at it, which I suppose confirms the topsyturvy values of the day.

One has to say though, that prisoner-of-war models generally are remarkable pieces of work considering the conditions under which they were apparently made. This applies particularly to the very small, all-wood models (unimaginatively called 'chipwood' models) where not only the guns and the deck fittings are made of wood, but all the sails and rigging as well, the rigging lines being strips of wood frequently as small as 1/400″ square in section. They are the pick of the bunch and a pleasure to restore.

It should also be said that the criteria applied to modern, accurate and realistic scale models should not apply to prisoner-of-war models. The fact that they are often over-sparred, over-rigged, under-bellied, not to scale, etc should perhaps be the required virtues, the looked-for characteristics of the good prisoner model.

Research It has been emphasized that the time spent at the bench doing the actual work is the item of prime importance. The time spent on research is a sacrifice of production time as is corresponding with and seeing the client. Perhaps what is needed is an industrious team of researchers to gather the information and an encouraging, enthusiastic and enterprising entrepreneur to take care of the sales. However, research must be done, for practical reasons never as much as one would like, and there is no knowing when all is done that can be done. Consequently one is left with the abiding apprehension that details may be wrongly shown or omitted on a model, and subsequently further information turns up long after it has been completed and exported abroad.

Frequently the information is just not in existence, this applies especially to the early periods and I am never really happy working on models prior to the seventeenth century. Hence the 'too-early' heading to the first chapter.

Even to do what one can necessitates skimming through a great deal of irrelevant matter, accounts of battles and voyages, log books and journals in the hope that a snippet of information on the physical appearance of the ship may result. The romance of the record passage is not for the ship model builder, he wants to know just where were the coaling scuttles of the *Great Western*, why are the Van de Velde drawings of the *Hampton Court*'s stern different from the original model of the ship in Wilton House, Salisbury, and just what did a mid-nineteenth-century marine journalist in Boston, Massachusetts, mean by pearl-colour?

However apart from the sometimes fruitless reading, one has the great pleasure of being able to study closely photos, prints, drawings and paintings of ships, and one comes to something of an appreciation of the great marine artists of the past, the Van de Veldes, Cleveleys, Charles Brooking, W. F. Mitchell and the amazing Roux family of Marseilles, with no one today nor in the recent past to touch them.

It is interesting to note too that the ship model builder's conception of a good marine painting is by no means the same as that of the nautical art expert; clouds of gunsmoke are all very well perhaps, but they just hide required detail and the vagueness of Turner becomes an abomination.

It so happens that I have specialized to some extent in two different fields: miniature Admiralty Board dockyard models of ships of the seventeenth-century Royal Navy, and waterline models of American clipper ships. I am glad to say the research for the latter is remarkably satisfactory.

The seventeenth-century vessels it is possible to copy have also proved quite numerous mainly as a result of the work of the Van de Veldes. However, here there is a most unfortunate situation, typical of model research, where we have a number of beautifully detailed drawings of named ships by these two artists showing clearly the figurehead, bow, the broadside, the quarter gallery, and sometimes even details of the athwartship bulkheads on deck but no indication of the stern, so that models cannot be made of them. As a further irritation there are a number of equally detailed stern views, but unnamed!

Obviously the named stern view is almost always of the greatest value, for then one usually gets a good idea of the broadside and, if one is lucky, in the far distance an indication of the figurehead, but even if the latter is not apparent a lion figurehead is fairly safe as the majority of ships of this period had them, even HMS *Tiger*.

The amateur modeller, like the professional, pays good money for photos of these drawings and paintings, also for photostats of draughts and for nautical books, and as this facet of costs is by no means as negligible as for materials, the professional has the advantage as these things are the tools of his trade and their cost therefore somewhat reduced by income tax relief.

However both parties, if of a like enthusiasm, have much both to gain in enjoyment of their prolonged contemplation, and to learn from them by the most painless means, that of automatic absorption.

The Illustrations The pictures in these pages are a small selection of the photographs of the models that I have taken, for record purposes, during the last twenty years or so. They are chosen to give the reader the maximum information about the models rather than for their quality or artistic merit, if any.

The inveterate ship modeller does well to acquire some small skill with the camera as photographing miniature models is something similar to the copy photographing of plans, documents and book pages, and to be able to do this is a great help in research.

Also the prospect of seeing a colour slide of say, a $1\frac{3}{4}''$-long Stuart Royal Yacht projected to fill a 4' square screen tends to keep one's standards of workmanship up to the mark, and one's opinion of it to a down-to-earth level!

Distribution Models Nos 1, 2, 3, 6, 7, 24, 33, 46, 48, 53, 59 and 60 together with other models of mine not described in these pages form the Cussons Collection, and are installed in the Maritime Museum, The Castle, Cape Town, SA.

Model No 22 is in the Colonial Williamsburg Museum, Virginia, USA.

The first of the six *Constitutions*, model No 27, is in the Smithsonion Institution, Washington, DC and the third is in the US Naval Academy Museum, Annapolis, Maryland, USA. To the best of my knowledge the remaining models are all in private collections throughout the world.

Dimensions The model lengths given in the following pages refer to extreme lengths including bowsprits, jibbooms, spanker booms, etc.

The New Deterrent It is with some distaste that I have to again refer to the new British sales tax (Value Added Tax) but I have to do so as these introductory notes are written, at least partly, for anyone intending to make his living at ship model building and this matter may have much bearing on what he is prepared to do, that is, if he is British.

Briefly, anyone registering for this tax is legally obliged to permit Customs and Excise Officers to enter his place of work from time to time; also he will have to fill up numerous forms once a quarter. The cost of the product is also increased of course.

Again briefly, to be legally exempt from this is to accept a fixed annual turnover together with other strictures which in themselves are so difficult to cope with as to make it only possible to build models of one's own choosing and offering these for sale to interested clients as and when permitted.

The erstwhile practice of accepting specific commissions is no longer possible under these restrictive measures.

1975   D. McN

I THE 'TOO-EARLY' MODELS

1. A Phoenician Galley (c700 BC)

Scenic model, scale 32'–1", 3" long

If the models in this book are to run in chronological order by the nature of things we have to start off with the earliest and therefore the most doubtful from a data source point of view.

There are a number of bas-reliefs on the walls of Sennacherib's palace at Nineveh. These were discovered by A. Layard in 1845, and they are reputed to be Phoenician galleys, dated at 700 BC – probably the only pictures of such vessels known.

In May 1952, M. I. Pliner, a naval architect of Nahariya, drew out a set of plans based on these carvings and gave the vessel a very broad midship section, taking the side of the upperworks up from the gunwales thus producing a very clumsy ship with considerable underwater resistance.

In 1961, Björn Landström in writing his book *The Ship* discovered that one of the reliefs showed that the arms of the oarsmen were outboard of the supports for the upperworks. This altered the whole conception of the construction of these galleys and consequently it has been possible to produce a much more workmanlike vessel with a very narrow central hull with typical apostis or outriggers built on the outside for the oars.

As usual with archaic portraits of ships the artists have no sense of scale or proportion and the galleys in the reliefs are shown much too short for their height and the human figures on them much too large and prominent. However, one of the carvings shows seventeen oars a side so, assuming the oarsmen's thwarts to be at 3' centres, this makes a length of 48' between the foremost and aftermost thwarts, and the fore and aft lengths outside of these can be roughly estimated to give a total overall of about 90'.

If it is reasonable to assume that the central hull was hollowed out from a single trunk, a tree some 90' in length with a diameter of at least 6' would be required.

The graceful canoe-like stern was probably of planked construction going to a point on the centre line, or it may have been a single thickness of planking. The embolon or ram was brass or bronze bound and must have been of considerable strength being as it was an integral part of the central hull. The upperworks platform, for the men-at-arms, was of light wickerwork construction suitable for such a narrow-beamed craft.

A short mast was stepped somewhat forward of amidships carrying a single square sail which could hardly have been used in anything but a stern wind.

The arrangement and working of oars on biremes, triremes, etc has been a matter of considerable and unresolved conjecture by the experts since time out of

mind. This model shows thwarts in the central hull for the men who worked the lower bank of oars which were run through holes in the apostis, the upper bank being manipulated by men sitting on thwarts in the apostis itself, these oars being pivoted through thong loops against thole pins in the edge of the gunwale. It would seem quite possible though that some galleys had their oars worked by standing oarsmen.

The galley is shown drawn up stern-first on a shingle beach, a tent has been pitched using five oars and a spare sail, various arms, spears, shields, bows and arrows are stacked nearby together with two sets of oars and the anchors and cables all above high-water mark. At the side of the tent is a group of amphorae (probably the most accurate things on the model as so many have been found by underwater archaeologists). One of these has tipped over, spilling red wine on the shingle near the smouldering camp fire.

This is my only scenic model, and as I never show human forms on the models this seemed to be the one way of getting over the difficulty of unmanned, exposed oars; and having the vessel beached avoided a number of other awkward uncertainties.

A perfectly good case could be made out for not even attempting to make models of such ancient craft where there is still so much more that one wants to know, and despite all the present-day underwater activity it is going to be a long time indeed before we know enough.

2. A Flemish Carrack (c1480)

Waterline model, scale 16′–1″, 8½″ long

This model represents a northern carrack of about 500 tons, length on the main deck 102′, breadth 34′, depth in hold 18′ and draught 13′.

The chief sources of information were the well-known engravings by the Flemish master 'W.A.' which show some of the most detailed pictures of medieval ships known. It may have been that 'W.A.' made his engravings from church votive models and not from actual ships, as he shows the exaggerated freeboard and unduly diminished underwater hull characteristic of these models.

As a result of the poor range of early swivel guns during the middle ages, naval tactics probably consisted largely of getting alongside the enemy and showering him with missiles from the mast tops and the raised fore and after castles. The shipwrights of the day must have been more concerned with building floating castles than good sea boats.

The grapnel at the bowsprit was thought to be used for the purpose of holding the enemy alongside and the pokes on the mast-top crane lines were undoubtedly used to replenish the top men's ammunition.

The tilt frames over the fore and after summercastles would be covered with stout netting in time of battle to afford some sort of protection to the crew and fighting troops carried on board. There are two steep casks on either quarter which were used for soaking the salt meat or fish. A member of the crew, called the shifter, had the duty of standing in these casks and helping the exudation of salt with his bare feet.

The heraldic devices on the knights' shields hanging along the pavise were mostly taken from a fourteenth-century illustration.

There are, of course, no existing plans contemporary with the ships of this period; indeed one wonders if plans were used in their actual construction, so we are again confronted with the problem of proportion. Were the ships really as round and tubby as 'W.A.' shows them or was this the artistic convention of the day?

The late R. Morton Nance was the great expert on this period and his various sketches and realizations in the early volumes of the *Mariner's Mirror* and elsewhere seem to show vessels of a more seaworthy appearance.

I know of only one model contemporary to this period and this is the remarkable votive *Mataro nao* now in the Prins Hendrik Museum in Rotterdam. It is very large and quite detailed in its rather rough and ready but somehow attractive fashion. It is so wide and deep for its short length that one gains an entirely spherical impression!

3. A Portuguese Caravel (c1500)

Waterline model, scale 32'–1", $3\frac{3}{8}$" long

The correct name for this vessel is a *caravela latina*, a caravel with fore and aft lateen sails and possibly Columbus's *Niña* originally looked like this. The other type of caravel was *caravela redonda* and was rigged with square sails.

A full-sized caravel was built and sailed across the Atlantic in 1962 and the voyage recorded in Robert Marx's book *The Voyage of the Niña II*. This is a most interesting account and gives a good idea what it was like for the early Portuguese navigators.

I have mentioned previously Björn Landström's excellent book *The Ship* which is an absolute mine of information especially for these early periods and his further book *Columbus* also has some good relevant illustrations. His workmanlike, sensibly proportioned and seaworthy-looking translations of the old contemporary drawings and carvings seem to me to be far and away the most believable yet done and one has the added bonus of the pleasurable contemplation of the quality of his draughtsmanship.

This model was made for the collection of models with South African historical interest and it is generally thought that the most frequently used type of vessel in early Portuguese navigation down the coast of Africa was the lateen-rigged caravel, with an approximate deck length of, say, 80', by today's standards small and inconvenient vessels for such long arduous voyages with such comparatively large complements.

The model is of such a ship, three-masted, armed with four bulwark swivel guns and two heavier pieces on the deck. The flag at the foremast staff is the Portuguese ensign of the period; the pennant and afterdeck bulwark shields show the divisions of this design.

With my own pet theory I like to trace the evolution of the bulwark shield up to the present day, starting with the round targes on the galleys of antiquity, and on the gunwales of the Viking ships. Then come the traditional-shaped shields with their significant heraldic devices.

In the seventeenth century these are replaced by the coloured arming cloths spread along the open rails – red with a white border for the English ships and plain red for the Dutch.

Next came the drab, black painted canvas over both rails and hammock nettings of the eighteenth and nineteenth centuries, until finally appear the immaculate white dodgers on the rails of our present royal yacht *Britannia*.

We could sum up the model builder's troubles with early ships by saying that he cannot maintain with any conviction that what he has done is correct because the necessary information does not exist.

On the same basis other people of course cannot say he is wrong, but this is of little comfort.

4. *Elizabeth Jonas* (c1598)
Elizabethan galleon

Waterline model, scale 32′–1″, 7½″ long

The sources for this model come basically from the draughts contained in the MSS preserved and entitled by Samuel Pepys 'Fragments of Ancient English Shipwrightry'. They consist of a number of coloured sheer elevations of various types, some sections and a rather sketchy spar plan. They are ascribed to the Elizabethan master-shipwright Matthew Baker and done possibly about 1586. It is thought that the largest ship shown in these documents represents the *Elizabeth Jonas* and the dimensions of the model agree reasonably well with the known dimensions of the ship.

The colourful decorations are taken from the draught. Curiously enough this formal geometrical design appears hardly at all on sixteenth-century artists' pictures of Elizabethan ships but has been used on all the so-called replicas built in modern times. I can't help feeling that all the *Golden Hinds*, the *Mayflowers*, the *Susan Constants*, etc are perhaps a little too decorative, bright and cheerful compared with their originals.

As with all these early ships there has to be a great deal of conjecture; there is no contemporary deck plan even; indeed one of our leading nautical experts has hazarded a guess that the galleon in Baker's MS may not represent a northern vessel at all but possibly a southern Mediterranean ship.

But I own to a partiality for this particular vessel as the large Science Museum model was the very latest creation of the museum workshops when I made my first teenage visits to South Kensington before the war, and was the pride and joy of the then curator Mr G. S. Laird Clowes. Also she was the subject of my very first Science Museum photograph. I have about 200 of them now and still maintain they are the best available from any museum.

Whatever can be said about the accuracy or otherwise of the original sources, such a model makes a very attractive and colourful picture and if all of Queen Elizabeth's navy looked like this I wish I had been there to see it.

2 THE SEVENTEENTH CENTURY

5. *Prince Royal* (1610)
50/60 gun, 3-decker

Waterline model, scale 32′–1″, $7\frac{1}{2}$″ long (colour plate p. 34)

From the point of view of data sources this model brings us on to firmer ground. As with most of the English seventeenth-century ships the bare basic dimensions appear in *Lists of Men-of-War* compiled by Dr R. C. Anderson, and the hull lines for this model were adapted from the *Treatise on Shipbuilding . . . 1620–1625*. Both these works are Occasional Publications of the Society for Nautical Research.

The masts, spars, sails and rigging were all worked out from Anderson's *The Rigging of Ships in the Days of the Spritsail Topmast*, subsequently republished as *Seventeenth Century Rigging*. Also there are six contemporary oil paintings of the *Prince Royal*. All show some inconsistency in the portrayal of the actual ship of course but they were of the greatest use. Three are by Adam Willaerts, one of which is at Windsor Castle, one at the National Maritime Museum, Greenwich and the third, at the time of building the model, was at the Gomshall Gallery, Guildford, Surrey.

The other three are all by Hendrik Cornelius Vroom; two of these (one at Hampton Court Palace and the other belonging to Mr Victor Montagu) from the photographs at least are rather dark and yield little, but the third Vroom at the Frans Hals Museum, Haarlem, is probably the best and certainly the most well known.

Willaerts has a habit of showing his ships remarkably close to land in order that he may introduce a great number of human figures on the shore. These are most interestingly shown and their dress and behaviour of such fascination that I fear more time than enough was spent quizzing them all in the photographs with a good strong lens.

It is quite remarkable what a total muddle both artists have made of the Royal Standard on five of the paintings. The mainmast flag on the Haarlem painting may perhaps represent a special occasion standard.

There is one other painting, the portrait of her builder Phineas Pett, which shows as a detail the stern of the ship in the process of being built. This is in the National Portrait Gallery, London.

The stout netting covering the exposed decks mentioned in reference to the carrack (model 2) had by this time been developed into wooden gratings and all the open decks except the after poop were roofed over with this material, a particularly difficult feature for the miniaturist. This was also the period of immensely complicated and fancy rigging. The veritable festoons of martnets on the lower sail leeches and the delightful many-toed crowsfeet on stays and

halyards must surely have been quite unnecessary.

The rigging on all these models is of painted wire, of many different diameters, some single-strand and some laid up either right- or left-handed as appropriate for its purpose. Also the rigging is actually built and assembled rather than rigged, reeved and roved as with soft materials like linen thread etc. Wire lends itself especially to the complications of this type of rigging as it can be made to hang in natural curves and stays as put. No amount of wet and dry, cold and warm days will make it stretch or shrink as constantly happens with soft rigging, and being of non-ferrous material it must be almost everlasting.

The model shows the *Prince Royal* with all her flags and pennants flying in a fresh breeze, hoisting her main topsail, towing astern her 27′ shallop and her 19′ jolly-watt. Her 51′ longboat or tender, with oars laid back and square sail lowering, is at the entry port.

6. *Haerlem* (c1640)
Dutch East Indiaman

Waterline model, scale 32′–1″, 5¾″ long (colour plate p. 33)

The earliest mention of the *Haerlem* in Dutch records was in 1639 and it seems likely that she was launched in that year. She was a Dutch East Indiaman of the Amsterdam Chamber, with a probable gun-deck length of about 130′ and must have been pierced for about forty carriage guns.

In her first year she performed the notable feat of sailing to Batavia in only 115 days without losing a single soul by scurvy or other disease. This good performance may be due to the fact that, being a good sailer and having no sick people on board, she could avoid calling at the Cape of Good Hope. So the *Haerlem* sailed right on to make the next best passage of the year.

In that same year of 1639 she was the flagship of Cornelis Symonsz van der Veer in the action off Goa on 30 September. This incident is generally known as the 'Surprisal of Goa's Bar'.

The *Haerlem* is shown in a painting of this action done by Hendrick van Anthonissen in the Rijks Museum, Amsterdam.

She subsequently made a number of voyages to Batavia, Penhoe, etc and on 21 December 1646 set sail for the former port with six other ships under the command of Jeremias van Vliet. On 25 March 1647 she went too close inshore at Table Bay, her captain tried to make her go round with the wind but this manoeuvre failed and she touched the ground in front of the Leeuwenberg not far from the Zoute river.

It proved impossible to get her off, her cargo was taken out and brought ashore, a small fortress was built some two miles from the river and called the Zandenborg, and here the cargo was stowed.

The *Haerlem*'s captain and some of the crew lived here until March 1648 when they and the remains of the cargo were taken home to Holland.

Since it was not until five years later that Jan van Riebeeck founded the Cape Settlement it may be said that the fortress of Zandenborg of 1647 was the first Dutch settlement in South Africa.

I am most indebted to Mr E. W. Petrejus, my old friend and a one time curator at the excellent Prins Hendrik Museum in Rotterdam, for his considerable help in supplying masses of historical and technical information not only for this model of the *Haerlem* but also for the pinasschip *Dromedaris*, the next to be dealt with. Indeed, I could not have done either model without his help.

Prior to building both these models my wife and I were afforded the fortunate opportunity of going to Holland to do the necessary research and numerous photographs were taken of the many seventeenth-century Dutch models in various museums.

Although not written in English, both Heinrich Winter's *Der Hollandische Zweidecker von 1660/1670* and Rolf Hoeckel's *Modellbau von Schiffen des 16. und 17. Jahrhunderts* were invaluable sources of information on European ships of the seventeenth century on account of their numerous and detailed illustrations.

In the Boymans Museum, Rotterdam, there is a drawing by Hans Savery (1597–1654) showing in very clear detail just such a ship as the *Haerlem* in very stormy conditions and the model follows this exactly. The top-gallant masts and the mizzen yards have been struck and stowed, the fore and main topsails furled and lowered to the caps, the fore course has its bonnet taken in and its yard correspondingly lowered. The main yard is aportlast and the mizzen lateen yard lowered almost to the deck.

7. *Dromedaris* (c1652)
Dutch pinasschip

Waterline model, scale 16′–1″, 7¼″ long

As is usual with ships of some historical significance little data remain regarding their precise appearance and dimensions.

The *Dromedaris* was Jan van Riebeeck's pinasschip which took the first permanent Dutch settlers to the Cape in 1652. She is an example of the particularly beautiful vessels made by the seventeenth-century Dutch shipbuilders: the wide forward beam, the graceful almost flamboyant sheer, and the carving finished in bright natural colours with little gilding are all characteristic of this period and country.

Almost the only written information is contained in Van Riebeeck's *daghregister* which he kept during the voyage from Holland to the Cape, and from this it appears that the *Dromedaris* was a pinasschip (although sometimes referred to as a yacht), that she had eighteen guns, two boats and carried topgallants.

Apparently she was a fairly fast sailer but lacked stability, as it is recorded on 20 February 1652 that nine of her guns had to be dismantled and placed in the hold. The remaining nine were housed in the gunroom, forecastle, steering

cuddy and on the main deck, facts which give us just a little more information about the ship herself.

In view of this dearth of specific detail it is fortunate that there are a number of pinasschip draughts in the Scheepvaart Museum, Amsterdam; these show single-decked vessels of eighteen guns and were apparently drawn in the middle of the seventeenth century, and like most draughts of this period are drawn in a primitive fashion, done free-hand perhaps and more pictorial than diagrammatic. Translating these to workmanlike drawings for practical application was perhaps one of the most difficult aspects of the model.

In the same museum is a contemporary model of a much larger pinas of two decks and pierced for twenty-eight guns. This model is probably of votive origin and is an exceptionally attractive seventeenth-century production, having a remarkably 'dry' appearance of great age compared with our own dockyard models glossy with varnish. It seems to have, undamaged, its original rigging and sails, the hull is studded with somewhat exaggerated treenails and it sports the curious wavy white waterline or boottooping which the best Dutch authorities assure me never appeared on the actual ships but only on their votive models.

The present *Dromedaris* model is based entirely on the eighteen-gun pinas hull draughts, the deck details from the works of Nicholaes Witsen and contemporary Dutch models, the mast and spar dimensions from Cornelis Van Yk, the decoration, rigging and many other details from the precise pen-paintings by the Elder Van de Velde.

The model shows the *Dromedaris* as she may have appeared in Table Bay on the completion of her voyage; her starboard anchor is down and the port one suspended on the cat falls half out of the water. Her flag arrangement is taken from the Alkmaar Museum painting of the homeward-bound East India fleet of Wollebrant Geleynsz de Jongh (1648), which incidentally included the ship *De Coninck van Polen* with Van Riebeeck on board.

Even in the Netherlands there seems to be some doubt as to just what is a pinasschip, but in the Scheepvaart Museum's 'Album of Plates of Ship Models & Draughts' the following is given: 'By "pinas" the seventeenth century understood the full-rigged three-masted ship whose planking, unlike that of a Dutch flute, ended at the stern in a square tuck.' This gives plenty of scope!

8. *Naseby* (1655)
80-gun, 3-decker

Admiralty Board dockyard model, scale 16′–1″, 12⅝″ long
(colour plate p. 33)

The *Naseby* was built under the Commonwealth by Mr Commissioner Pett at Woolwich in 1655. Her dimensions were: length by the keel 131′, beam 42′, depth in hold 18′, tons burden 1230. Her armament was a maximum of 86 guns reduced in peace time to 76.

John Evelyn recorded in his diary on 9 April 1655: 'I went to see the great ship newly built by the Usurper, Oliver, carrying 96 brass guns, and 1000 tons burden. In the prow was Oliver on horseback, trampling six nations under foot, a Scot, Irishman, Dutchman, Frenchman, Spaniard and English as was easily made out by their several habits. A fame held a laurel over his insulting head: the word "God with us".'

Edward Barlow recorded in his journal that upon serving as a boy on the *Naseby*: 'I was put into a cabin to sleep a thing much like a Gentleman's dog kennel, for I was forced to creep in upon all fours, and when I was in and set upon my breech I could not hold my head upright.'

The *Naseby* was Montagu's flagship in the Restoration fleet which brought Charles II back from Holland in 1660, and when the King stepped aboard he renamed her the *Royal Charles* (see model 12). She saw action at Lowestoft in 1665, the Four Days' Battle and the St James's Day Fight in 1666. In 1667 the Dutch captured her in the Medway and carried her off to Holland where she was finally broken up in 1673.

There are a number of Van de Velde drawings of the *Naseby/Royal Charles* at the National Maritime Museum, Greenwich, the Boymans Museum, Rotterdam and the Scheepvaart Museum, Amsterdam, and there is also a drawing by Storck in the Rijks Museum, Amsterdam. There are also several contemporary paintings by Barlow, Bakhuizen, Van Diest, Van Soest and others, together with a long and detailed description of the *Royal Charles* by the Dutch shipwright, Nicholaes Witsen. All the above were used in the construction of the model.

As this is the first of a number of Admiralty Board dockyard models in this book some explanation must be given regarding this traditional English form of model building. During the seventeenth and early part of the eighteenth centuries it was customary for the Admiralty shipwrights to make large models of the naval vessels they were about to build. These models were usually unrigged and to a scale of $4'-1''$.

They were built in a particular conventional way showing the timbers of the hull in stylized fashion with the planking omitted below the wales and only a small amount of planking shown on the decks.

It is generally believed that this method was devised to allow the King and the members of the Navy Board to inspect the interior arrangements of the decks etc, on the assumption that they would be unable to read a shipwright's draught. This explanation may be true. I do not know its original source but it could equally well be said that this just happened to be the way they built ship models at this period and that the vertical lines of the exposed timbers showed up the hull form to perfection, better than any other method. No other country built ship models quite in this style and our earliest known examples date back to about 1650. It is interesting to note that the earlier the date the less planking appears on the hull and decks.

There are two known unplanked seventeenth-century dockyard models: the 2-decker, dated 1655, at Greenwich and the model in the Stockholm Museum traditionally known as *Sheldon's Naseby*. (A large model of the *Loyal London* of 1666 was destroyed when Trinity House, London was bombed on 29 December 1940.)

(Bottom) *Haerlem* scale 32'–1" 5¾" long (see p. 26)
(Top) *Naseby* scale 16'–1" 12⅝" long (see opposite page)

Prince Royal scale 32′–1″ 7½″ long (see p. 24)

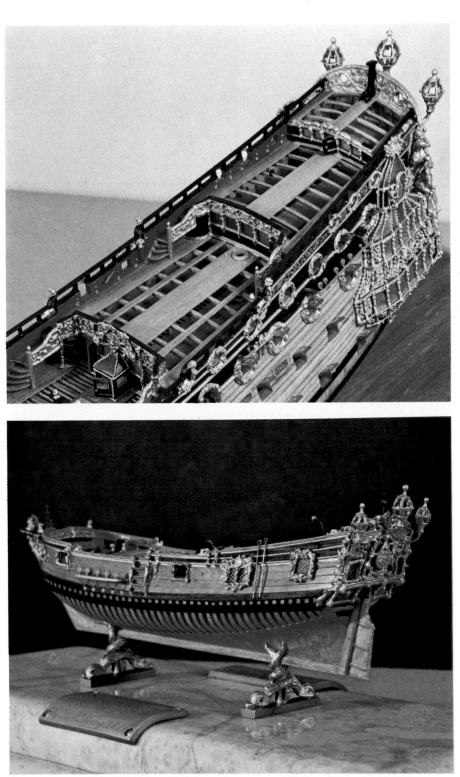

(Bottom) HMY *Kitchen* scale 16′–1″ 5¼″ long (see p. 56)
(Top) HMS *Britannia* scale 16′–1″ 13⅛″ long (see p. 64)

HMS *Resolution*   scale 16′–1″   11½″ long   (see p. 51)

(Opposite top) HMS *Queen Charlotte*   scale 32′–1″   9¾″ long   (see p. 80)
(Opposite bottom) *Constitution*   scale 16′–1″   18½″ long   (see p. 84)

HMS *Medway*   scale 16′–1″   14¾″ long   (see p. 74)

HMS *Brunswick* scale 16′–1″ 13⅛″ long (see p. 82)

HMY *Mary*   scale 16′–1″   6¼″ long   (see opposite page)

Francis Sheldon was a shipwright concerned with the building of the *Naseby* at Woolwich. He went to Gothenburg in 1658 as a master shipwright in the service of the King of Sweden and apparently took this model with him. The dimensions and armament arrangements agree fairly well with the *Naseby* so it may perhaps be her original dockyard model, although some of the experts do not agree. However, this model in Sweden is a most interesting one for many reasons but its unique feature is a cockpit in the after end of the quarter deck, a cockpit very like those we shall come across in the royal yachts of a slightly later date.

If one is to use this model as a basis for the *Naseby* (the Stockholm Museum has an excellent set of lines taken off the model) this cockpit has to be reconciled with the quite detailed exteriors shown by the contemporary artists, and this has been done on the model.

As has been said the hull timbers of dockyard models are stylized. The timbers of the actual ships were not like this at all and in future models we shall encounter interesting variations of timbering.

This model of the *Naseby* shows a very open style of framing with only one solid, overlapping band of doubling along the hull at the level of the main wales. All the upper timbering is made to taper as it goes upwards and from a ship model building point of view this must be the second most difficult form of dockyard model building. There is another system shown in photographs of the *Loyal London* model mentioned above where the frames are free-standing with no continuous belt and are connected only by the wales and mouldings. This I have not yet tried.

The model bears the Commonwealth carving shown in such great detail in the Van de Velde drawings and the Cromwell figurehead described by Evelyn. The dolphin stands supporting the model incorporate the two badges of the Commonwealth, the Cross of St George and the Irish Harp.

It is recorded that dockyard models were made before the 1650s but none are known to have survived, and no one now knows what they looked like, how they were built or what curious conventions were observed in their construction.

9. HMY *Mary* (1660)
8-gun, Royal Yacht

Waterline model, scale 16′–1″, 6¼″ long (colour plate p. 40)

The *Mary* was built at Amsterdam originally for the Dutch East India Company but was presented by the Dutch to Charles II at his restoration. She can thus claim to be the first English Royal Yacht.

She is a typical Dutch production with a shallow draught, large lee boards and the usual commodious accommodation astern.

I know of three contemporary pictures of her by the Younger Van de Velde,

Storck and Beerstraten. All of these show a unicorn for the figurehead and the Stuart Royal Arms on the stern so one imagines that the Dutch must have had these done especially for Charles. There is also a contemporary plan in Witsen of a very similar yacht.

Some of her fittings and materials from a contemporary list make fascinating reading: one copper horn for the figurehead, 1013 little books of gold, 12 linden timbers for carving, 49½ yards of gold leather, silk taffeta red, blue and white for standards and pennants. Mast 100 guilders, topmast (lashed on) 12 guilders, gaff 22 guilders, bowsprit with knee 8 guilders, lower yard 5 guilders, topsail yard 4 guilders and finally a 12′ long scoop for wetting the sails.

The *Mary* is shown under full sail, the Royal Standard at the masthead and the peculiarly Dutch fitting of a flag staff at the gaff peak occupied by a small Union flag.

10. HMS *Royal Escape* (1660)
4-gun smack

Admiralty Board and waterline models, scale 16′–1″, 4″ long

One of the most important ships in English history was a small, insignificant collier smack called the *Surprise* owned by Captain Nicholas Tattersall of Brighton, Sussex. She was probably built during the 1640s at Shoreham and was quite small with a keel length of 30′ 6″, a beam of 14′ 3″, a draught of 7′, a tonnage of 34 and a crew of four men and a boy.

The irregular wanderings of Charles II after the disastrous battle of Worcester eventually brought him and his companions to Shoreham and in the very early morning of 15 October 1651 they quietly boarded the *Surprise* and set sail for Poole Harbour, later altering their course for France and eventually anchoring two miles off shore at Fécamp. Charles and his companion, Viscount Wilmot, were rowed ashore in the *Surprise*'s cock-boat. One of the oarsmen, Richard Carver, had the distinction of being the last of many to help the King by carrying him ashore on his shoulders.

At his restoration in 1660 the King set about rewarding the friends who had helped him. Tattersall did very well. The King gave him a command in the Royal Navy and bought the *Surprise* from him, entered her in the Navy, had her refitted at Deptford and renamed her *Royal Escape*. She was armed with four very small guns and her crew appropriately increased.

For over ten years the *Royal Escape* was used as one of the King's personal vessels and was generally moored off Whitehall Palace, perhaps as a reminder to his subjects of the use he had to make of her originally.

Although she was such a small ship neither pains nor expense were spared in her fitting out as is shown in the following extract from one of the warrant books of the Great Wardrobe:

To the Right Honble. Ralph Montague,
  Master of His Majesties Great Wardrobe
  or to his Deputy.
  These are to signify unto you his Majesties Pleasure that you provide & deliver or cause to be provided & delivered unto Luke Wilks Esq. yeoman of His Majesties removing wardrobe of bedds.
  These particulars following for his majesties Service in his vessell the 'Royal Escape' – viz., One dozen of Turkey worke chairs, one dozen of Turkey worke cushions, Four Quilted Bedds, Two small Feather bedds, Six feather Pillows, Six Coverlet Quilts, Six pairs of White Blankets, Two small Turkey worke carpetts, Two small curtacices, Four Pewter Candlesticks, Two Pewter Chamberpotts and Two pair of Snuffers. And this shall be your warrant given under my hand this xxiiii day of September in xxiiii year of his Majesties Reign.

St Alban

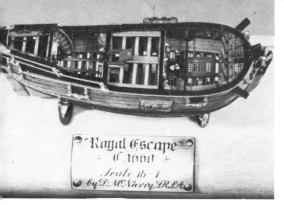

"Royal Escape"
C.1660
Scale 16-1
by D. McNarry, A.R.P.S.

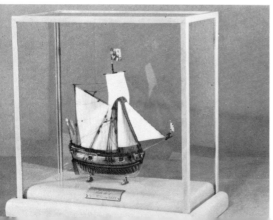

One can't help wondering where they found room for all this on such a small boat!

The *Royal Escape* was handed over to the Navy for general service in 1673 and was rebuilt in 1714.

These models are based on the recorded dimensions and the various pictures done by the Younger Van de Velde. The latter consist of two drawings and an oil portrait in the National Maritime Museum, Greenwich, one drawing in the British Museum, and a further excellent oil portrait in Her Majesty's collection at Buckingham Palace. The dockyard model versions show one of the variations in hull framing used in the building of Admiralty Board models, that of complete alternate frames and spaces for models of smaller vessels. However, it is most unlikely that a dockyard model was ever made of the *Surprise* even when she was refitted for royal use. The two oil paintings and the three drawings mentioned above all agree well enough together and there is no doubt they do show the *Royal Escape*.

However there is another Van de Velde drawing at Greenwich, marked (in Dutch) 'Royal Escape'. This is of an altogether different vessel with five square ports a side instead of two and it has been suggested that this might be the smack *Tower*. Unfortunately there is a large-scale museum model purporting to be the *Royal Escape* and seemingly made from this one drawing alone. An example of the perils of research.

The two lower illustrations show typical, if small, examples of the two types of glass case in which all the models are mounted. The design of plain rounded moulding is the same for every model and was originally conceived to produce the simplest appearance possible so as not to detract the eye from the model; but like most things which look simple they are not simple to make. A considerable variety of veneers is used, the two examples here being of light plain sycamore.

11. Royal Yachts (17th century)

Waterline models, scales 16', 32' and 64'–1", 7", $3\frac{1}{2}$" and $1\frac{3}{4}$" long

This group of royal yachts shows immediately the great difference between English-built yachts and the Dutch built *Mary* (model 9).

The reaction of English shipwrights seems to have been to discard the high stern cabin and the lee boards and to produce sleeker vessels of deeper draught much like very small 6th rates (see explanation under model 13).

The necessary head height in the after cabins was obtained by some ingenious stepping of the decks and entry was usually made via a small cockpit.

Our Dutch friend Witsen, surveying the *Katherine* after her capture, describes going down an ornate stairway to two rooms aft. The first was a hall painted all round with works of art, gilded and decorated with carvings, the other was lavishly panelled with an inlaid floor and containing a four-poster bed. The inside of the stern windows were decorated with gold leatherwork.

The first of the yachts shown here is this same *Katherine* built at Deptford in 1661 and the first Royal Yacht built specifically for the King. She had a keel length of 49' and a 19' beam, and an armament of eight small cannon, probably 3-pounders. A feature of the rigging of these single-masted Stuart yachts was the freedom of both yards: neither of them being attached to the mast with the usual parrels, their weight being taken by the halyards and lifts, with the braces of the lower yards only holding them back to the mast.

The *Katherine* conveyed the King on the royal visit to the fleet on 5 June 1672 after the Battle of Solebay and is depicted in the well-known painting of this occasion. She was captured by the Dutch at the Battle of Texel in 1673 but later returned as a gift by William of Orange and used by the Ordnance Office.

The model shows the *Katherine* as she appeared after capture by the Dutch wearing the flags and pennant of the City of Amsterdam. There is a Van de Velde painting of her under these conditions in the Scheepvaart Museum, Amsterdam.

The yacht in the upper pair of pictures is the *Charles* of 1675, again of 8 guns, built at Rotherhithe and at half the scale of the *Katherine*.

There are five Van de Velde drawings of this yacht, three rather faint but the other two clear and detailed: one, a bow view with broadside, and the other a stern view with broadside – both ideal from the model builder's point of view.

Unfortunately the figurehead is cut off in the former drawing but can be seen to be an equestrian figure surrounded by cherubs etc in one of the other drawings. The *Charles* was wrecked in 1678.

The two lower pictures show typical yachts, again to half the scale.

To the best of my knowledge there are six original seventeenth-century yacht models of the single-masted rig. The lines have been taken off two of these and plans are available at Kensington and Greenwich. Also there are the two detailed sheer elevation drawings inboard and outboard in Coronelli's 'Gli Argonauti Atlante Veneto' (1693), which are both for ketch yachts. The inboard one shows the interior arrangements in great detail.

Royal Yacht. c1680.

Royal Yacht c1670.

12. HMS *Royal Charles* (c1666)
80-gun, 3-decker

Waterline model, scale 64′–1″, $3\frac{5}{8}$″ long

This is of course the *Naseby* (see model 8) in her Restoration state and much the same data sources were used with the addition of the masts and rigging etc worked out from Anderson.

Samuel Pepys recorded in his diary on 14 December 1663: 'But, among other things, Lord! what an account did Sir J. Minnes and Sir W. Batten make of the pulling down and the burning of the head of the "Charles" where Cromwell was placed with people under his horse, and Peter, as the Duke called him, is praying

to him: and Sir J. Minnes would needs infer the temper of the people from their joy at the doing of this and their building a gibbet for the hanging of his head up, when God knows, it is even the flinging away of £100 out of the King's purse, to the building of another, which it seems must be a Neptune.'

As far as I know there is no contemporary picture showing the new figurehead, but the Van Diest painting shows a rear view of something very like a seahorse, so the figurehead on this model was designed on the basis of the charioted Neptune drawn by two seahorses shown in the very beautiful drawing of the *Triumph* by the Younger Van de Velde.

The original carving of the Royal Arms carried on the stern of the *Royal Charles* is preserved in the Rijks Museum, Amsterdam. There are very few pieces of Caroline ships' carving extant and this must be one of the most important examples remaining. When my wife and I were in Holland researching for the Dutch models we examined the carving very carefully. Unfortunately it was then mounted high up on a wall over an open archway between two galleries in the museum. We wished to measure its width, of course, so we dropped a couple of lines to the floor from as far up as we could reach and then measured the floor. As I remember, the museum was rather full at the time and this procedure occasioned the raising of the odd Dutch eyebrow, but we discovered that the carving's extreme width was 12′ 1″. I later obtained a large photo and proportioned out the rest of the measurements. On this model at 64′–1″ the stern arms are $\frac{3}{16}$″ wide.

Some of the paint still adheres, rather faded, to the original carving and it is interesting to note that on the actual ships, and thus on realistic waterline models, the Royal Arms and sometimes other heraldic insignia are painted in full colour, but these are always just gilded on dockyard models.

Happily enough this model was made for a descendant of General George Monk, later Duke of Albemarle, who sailed in the *Naseby* in May 1660 to collect Charles II from Holland at the Restoration. Monk also commanded her and the fleet at the Four Days' Battle in 1666 and this model shows the ship on this occasion with his flag, a Union, at the mainmast. The lower tier of ports are closed, the staysails furled, the topgallant masts are not rigged and the mainsail is clewed up.

I never have the least doubt in my own mind that very small-scale models like this are of much greater worth than a similar model at say, 16′–1″. If the normal amount of detail is to be included it requires a great deal more care and skill to produce this and a totally different standard of work is involved.

Perhaps this is an appropriate place to mention that all the models in this book (excepting only the 100′–1″ modern warship models) have their decks properly planked with separate planks, the hulls of the wooden vessels are similarly planked and the hulls of the iron and steel ships are plated to scale. In some instances I have tried scoring the deck planking for dockyard models simply because this was sometimes done, rather lazily, on the original large-scale models but I do not find it satisfactory on miniature work.

13. HMS *Resolution* (1667)

70-gun, 3rd rate, 2-decker

Admiralty Board dockyard model, scale 16′–1″, 11½″ long
(colour plate p. 37)

The *Resolution* was built by Sir Anthony Deane at Harwich in 1667. The information for the model's construction was gathered from the known and recorded dimensions, the draughts and data contained in Deane's *A Doctrine of Naval Architecture* (1670) and the drawings and painting of the actual ship by Willem Van de Velde the Younger.

Samuel Pepys was quite largely concerned with the building of the *Resolution* and mentions her several times in his diaries. Also he had a 'draft' of the ship, a present from his friend Deane 'set up . . . to my extraordinary content' in his house at Seething Lane.

This is the second model of this ship I have made and is unusual in that it was made for a very special purpose which in the end came to nought. This model was intended as an anonymous gift for permanent installation in a public building which has special connections with Samuel Pepys, but the dead hand of the Value

Added Tax, falling even upon freely donated gifts, frustrated this intention.

So far this is the only armed dockyard model I have made and it was surprisingly difficult to install the guns, much more so than on an ordinary full hull model, and involved an almost continuous process of fitting and removing and refitting the guns as the inboard work was done.

The seventy guns – twenty-six demi-cannon, twenty-six 12-pounders, sixteen lite sakers and two 3-pounders – were all made before the model was started and took, neatly enough, seventy hours to do; four minutes to turn, bore and complete each barrel and the remaining fifty-six minutes spent on the planked cheeks, beds, quoins, trucks, trunnions, etc including the final assembly of all these. The demi-cannon on the gun deck have their muzzles fitted with red and white tampions, the remainder are left open.

On the old original dockyard models the guns, if found at all, are usually of rather a poor quality, especially the carriages, so I fear the guns on this model are perhaps too detailed.

We have met the word 'rate' before in these pages and I hasten to say that 3rd rate does not mean a poor quality ship. The actual word comes from the rates of pay for officers which was dependent upon the classification of the ship. During the seventeenth and eighteenth centuries ships of the Royal Navy were classified by rates according to the number of guns and decks. Consequently the changes that were effected from time to time make the whole matter quite confusing.

The model is mounted in a case of satin-finished English oak on a shelf of the same timber. The dolphin stands supporting the hull embody the arms of the Pepys family and the ornamental bosses of the screws securing the case to the shelf are cold brass castings with the diarist's initials in relief together with appropriate devices enamelled in full colour.

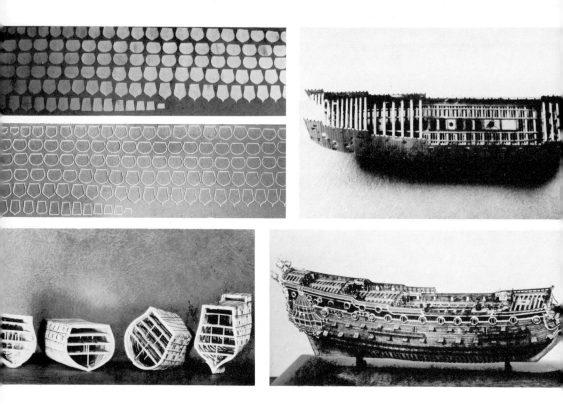

14. HMS *Prince* (1670)
100-gun, 1st rate, 3-decker

Admiralty Board dockyard model, scale 32′–1″, $6\frac{3}{8}''$ long

From a model builder's point of view the *Prince* is probably the most well known of seventeenth-century ships. More modern models must have been built of her (and certainly more started!) than any other ship of this period mainly because, in 1938, the Science Museum produced a set of lines from the original model.

This model was apparently bought by the Science Museum in 1895 and was unrigged. Three years later it was rigged very badly indeed and for some reason was then known as the *Royal Charles*. Subsequently it was re-rigged correctly and the final identification established as the original model for the 1st-rate HMS *Prince* built by Phineas Pett at Chatham in 1670. To my mind it is the finest and most attractive of our dockyard models and is now well displayed at the Science Museum.

One curious feature is that the central part of the rail at the break of the quarter deck is missing. There seems to be no evidence that it was removed, rather that it was just not made in the first place. Various theories have been advanced, none entirely satisfactory. Normally the rail would continue straight across the quarterdeck and more often than not would be embellished with a large Royal Arms or a badge with supporters in the middle.

There is little doubt that the present identification of the model is correct but there is a variation in the stern shown in some of the contemporary pictures. The *Prince* was probably built with a plain closed stern as shown on the model and in the Van de Velde 'Royal Visit to the Fleet' painting of 1672. However in the Jan van Beecq portrait of 1679 at Greenwich and in two Van de Velde drawings – one in the Rijks Museum and the other in the Boymans Museum – a small, projecting open gallery is shown at the level of the upper deck, its extent covering the three central windows only, the middle one of which must have been converted to a doorway.

L. G. Carr-Laughton in his *Old Ship Figure-Heads and Sterns* calls this kind of gallery a 'dicky'. When I did the first of my two models of the ship, at 50′–1″ nearly a quarter of a century ago, I only had the Rijks drawing and it puzzled me greatly.

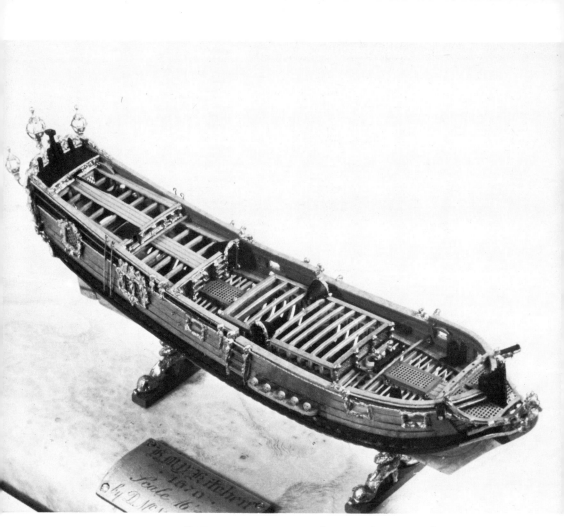

15. HMY *Kitchen* (1670)
6-gun Royal Yacht

Admiralty Board dockyard model, scale 16′–1″, 5¼″ long
(colour plate p. 35)

Length of keel 51′, beam 19′ 4″ and built by William Castle at Rotherhithe. She was probably armed with six 3-pounders and carried a crew of thirty who earned £4 per man per month but were lucky if they were paid it.

It is generally believed that the King had the *Kitchen* specially designed and built to carry the royal cooks and servants during his various yachting cruises. She was certainly used as a cookhouse vessel as there is a drawing in the Boymans Museum, Rotterdam, with an inscription to the effect that on 16 July 1673 the King's food was being taken in a wherry from the *Kitchen* to the *Cleveland*, another Royal Yacht. However in view of the fact that she was obviously built to the same ornate standards as normal royal yachts and must have had very roomy accommodation below the raised deckhead on the main deck, it is possible that she served as a dining saloon vessel as well. The *Kitchen* was made a Bomb in 1692 and sold out of the service in 1698.

One of the five drawings of the yacht shows her at a most unusual and useful angle heeling towards the artist who must have been at the poop rail of a much larger vessel, looking down on her decks.

The model shows a further variation in the timbering, this time arranged to give completely solid floors over the keel. I find it an interesting speculation to wonder just what these Admiralty Board models looked like when they were new 300 years ago.

Two of the earliest models, the Greenwich two-decker dated 1655 and the Stockholm model, present a dark appearance as apparently did the destroyed *Loyal London*. This may be due to extra old age or perhaps they were finished differently. Most of the dockyard models however are of a very warm tan colour, the varnish and the timber too, presumably, having mellowed with time.

Whilst pear and other woods sometimes occur on the models I always have the impression that box and lime were the most frequently used woods, and if one imagines these light yellow-cream timbers freshly finished with clear varnish the effect must have been quite different from what we see today. The models would have had a bright pale-golden appearance and must have looked very fine indeed.

No wonder Pepys recorded on 12 August 1662, 'Mr. Deane. . . . promises me also a modell of a ship which will please me exceedingly, for I do want one of my owne.'

I have often wished to produce such a model myself but the limitation in variety of timber of precise thickness prevents it.

16. HMS *James-Galley* (1676)
30-gun, galley frigate

Waterline model, scale 32'–1", $4\frac{7}{8}''$ long

Both the *James-Galley* and her consort the *Charles-Galley* were built on the Thames in the same year, both carried 30/32 guns, mostly sakers, both were originally 4th rates but were later reduced to 5th rates, and each had a crew of approximately 200 men.

The *James* was the smaller of the two but both were something of an innovation. It seems that in an attempt to protect their underwater hulls with an early form of sheathing, lead plating was used, and one would not imagine it being very successful.

Both ships were designed to combat the ravages of the Barbary pirates on the English merchant fleets. Apparently they did not come up to expectations in this respect as Jeremy Roch, who commanded the *Charles-Galley* c1690 recorded that with forty-two oars and three men to each they could only make three miles per hour. However they were apparently much better under sail as he also mentions

that as they were the best sailer in the fleet ''twas fit she should bring up the rear'.

We can gain some idea of what life was like on a small warship of the period from this entry in Roch's journal in which he complains about the foul humid atmosphere: 'The occasion of these damps is the tightness of a ship and, lying still a long time, the bilge water corrupts and stinks so that it is enough to poison the Devil, and all the little plate and silver I had hath been turned black with the vapours of our bilge waters in a night's time. Upon which I made the carpenter bore a plug hole to let in water now and then to clense it, and so pump it out again which in a little time did the business.'

There are four Van de Velde drawings of the *James-Galley*: two at Greenwich, one in the Victoria and Albert Museum and one at the Boymans Museum in Rotterdam. Of the *Charles-Galley* there is a drawing and an oil painting at Greenwich and another painting in a private French collection.

Jeremy Roch did a rather primitive but useful watercolour of his ship. There is also the external sheer elevation plan, a typical pictorial product of the period showing the athwartship shape of the lower timbers along the entire length of the profile.

The *James-Galley* was at one time commanded by Sir Cloudesley Shovell and

58

the following is an extract from his log dated 23 June 1683: 'Before 3 a clock in ye morning, Severall of ye Spanish Armado anchored near us, 3 of ym about 70 gunns a piece, lay within pistoll shott of us, and So placed ym selves yt we could not cast our Ship. without being a board of one of them, they sent on board to demand a Salute, and being denyed twice, they fired a grate gunn, and a Vally of small Shott ye genls Ship not being fitted to Come down, had put himselfe a board ye Vise admll of the Flanders Squadron, I saw his Majtys Ship and Subjects in Such Unavoydable Danger of being destroyed thought twas better to redeem Ship and lives. with a Salute than Ruen the whole.'

Apparently the King thought wrong had been done him but was not dissatisfied with Shovell.

The model shows the *James-Galley* in an almost flat sea with her sweeps out and the sails and flags hanging limp in the still air.

With a good deal of time and gentle persuasion one can make becalmed sails look reasonably realistic but I have yet to halfway satisfy myself with sails set and full of wind. To try and make a flat sheet of suitable material belly out appropriately in the middle without crinkling the edges seems, so far, to be a totally defeating process.

17. HMS *Grafton* (1679)
70-gun, 3rd rate, 2-decker

Waterline model, scale 16′–1″, 13⅜″ long

The original dockyard model of the *Grafton* once belonged to the artist J. Seymour Lucas and after his death was bought by Colonel H. H. Rogers and is now in the US Naval Academy Museum at Annapolis. I have photos of the model as owned by Lucas which show it to be in a very poor condition, both head and stern completely missing. It has now been restored and rigged out of all recognition and it is probably impossible to tell what is original and what is new.

Dr Anderson examined the model thoroughly in about 1912 and is responsible for its identification. The gun deck and beam measurements together with the armament agree reasonably well with the known data on the *Grafton*, and a section of the known original carving on the model shows, at the break of the quarter deck, the arms adopted by George Legge when he became first Baron Dartmouth in 1682. These arms incorporate those of the Washington family as Legge's mother, Elizabeth, was a Washington.

Dartmouth was appointed Admiral of the Fleet for the expedition to evacuate Tangier in 1683 and the *Grafton* was his flagship. At the King's express request Samuel Pepys went along as 'Wise Councellor' and left his impressions in the Tangier Papers.

As far as I know there is only one Van de Velde drawing of the *Grafton*.

The model shows the ship wearing the Admiral's Union flag at the main and hoisting her topgallant. The traditional red and white arming cloths are spread

along the waist and are furled elsewhere.

All the waterline and the ordinary full hull models which have concealed decks pierced with open gunports etc obviously have to be made hollow, so these models are carved and hollowed out from two pieces of timber and the interior decks and necessary fittings are all included before the two halves are finally joined together at the centreline. I lay some stress on the word 'necessary' here; every inboard item that can be glimpsed through ports, windows and hatches is, of course, included but nothing unnecessary is fitted. One has to be quite firmly realistic and practical about this, much as one might like to play around with interior decorations. I have little time for the modeller who laboriously panels out and furnishes the after cabin of HMS *Whatnot* and then covers in the whole thing so that no one can see it. It is a waste of the model builder's time and from a professional point of view a waste of the client's money as he pays for what he can neither see nor appreciate.

18. HMS *Tiger* (1681)
46-gun, 4th rate, 2-decker

Admiralty Board dockyard model, scale 16′–1″, 9⅜″ long

The *Tiger* was rebuilt from an earlier vessel of that name of 1647. Launched at Deptford in 1681 she had a length by the keel of 104′, a beam of 32′8″ and was 590 tons burden. On 17 August of that year Charles II paid a special visit to the new ship, then lying off Woolwich, before she sailed for the Mediterranean. She was then under the command of Lord Charles Berkeley of Stratton who died on board the following year.

The *Tiger* was rebuilt again in 1702 to slightly larger dimensions and yet again in 1722, but this term 'rebuilt' which occurs so often in the lists of the men-of-war probably meant very little. It is unlikely that much of the fabric of the old ship went into the new one; possibly it was just a convention preferable to indicating the building of a new ship.

The *Tiger* had a neat arrangement of sweep ports: one either side of the gunports on the gun deck and across the stern a single row of five windows with three large panels above, the central one with the usual Stuart arms and those either side with carvings of two tigers facing inwards; but the figurehead, notwithstanding the ship's name, is the usual lion.

The Van de Velde drawings, there are nine all told, show the *Tiger* in great detail and were probably done at the time of the royal visit mentioned above. There are also two excellent oil paintings of her at Berkeley Castle, Gloucestershire.

The method of framing in this model could perhaps be called the normal method as it is more frequently found than any other. It consists of two bands of doubling each side, the upper at the main wales and the lower at the turn of the bilge. Several interesting theories have been advanced in the *Mariner's Mirror* regarding the significance or otherwise of the arrangement of the conventional timbering on models. It may be that the fore and aft thickness of the timbers represents 'room and space' and the sheering lines of doubling futtock ends on the ship, or perhaps the cutting down or rising lines on the draught, or again perhaps it was just simply a nice looking way of doing it.

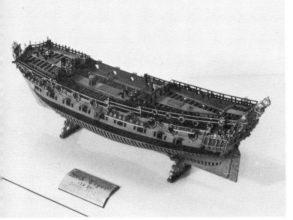 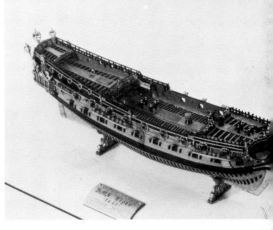

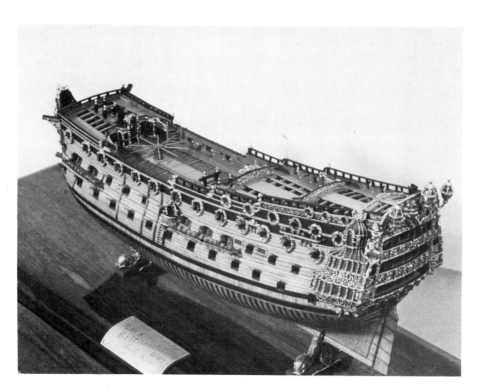

19. HMS *Britannia* (1682)

100-gun, 1st rate, 3-decker

Admiralty Board and waterline models, scale 16′–1″, 13⅛″ (colour plate p. 35) and 15¼″ long

Once in the Charles Sergison Collection at Cuckfield Park, Sussex, and now in the Rogers Collection at the US Naval Academy Museum, Annapolis, is a large model of a 3-decker of 100 guns.

As a result of my specializing somewhat in building seventeenth-century dockyard models I have also been working intermittently on a catalogue of the known Admiralty Board models of the period 1650–1705, collating all the published photos and writings about each model and there is no doubt at all that more has been written and published about this particular model than any other of the period. It seems to have been a matter of great fascination to all the experts, especially in the more interesting early volumes of the *Mariner's Mirror*, as to whether or not it is the *Britannia* and, if it is, which *Britannia*, that of 1682 or some slightly dubious version of 1700.

The model at Annapolis has the name 'Britania' (one 'n' for symmetry's sake) in the carving at the break of the aftermost deck. Some of its other carving, notably the figurehead and the taffrail, agree very well with contemporary pictures but most of the other decoration is in a later style than 1682.

One also has to pick one's way with care through the contemporary pictures of

the ship. There are two similar paintings of her, both apparently by Isaac Sailmaker, one at Greenwich and the other of unknown whereabouts. In the 1947
National Maritime Museum Guide there is listed an oil of the *Britannia* with a
queried attribution to the Younger Van de Velde. From the photograph it is a
fine, useful picture but I have never been able to catch a glimpse of the original
painting and it has such an interesting query about the stern which might be
resolved by looking at the real thing.

There was a rumour that there was another painting of her in the collection of
the Earl of Mount Edgcumbe but I could find no photo of it after a long day's
search in the Courtauld Institute of Art and it subsequently transpired that the

noble Earl himself had no record of it.

Coronelli, of 'Gli Argonauti' fame, comes on to the scene with a set of eight semi-diagrammatic, semi-pictorial drawings all probably taken from a model but somehow all lack the simple practical requirements of completeness and consistency; his line drawing shows only the hull form up to the lower wales and is very difficult to use.

Fortunately there are the 'safe' Van de Velde drawings; two at Greenwich and one at Boymans Museum, the broadside drawing being of particular use.

Of the ship herself we are on reasonably safe ground. Her dimensions were length on the gun deck 165′ 5″, beam 47′ 4″ (later girdled to 48′ 4″), depth in hold 18′, tons 1708. She was built at Chatham by Phineas Pett in 1682 and was the largest and possibly the most ornate warship of her time.

Her complement was approximately 780 men and her armament ranged from 42-pounders down to 3-pounders.

In 1688, Pepys, Deane and Hewer had occasion to go down to Gillingham Reach to inspect the fleet and stayed to a treat of cold meats and a bowl of punch on board the *Britannia*, as Bryant has it 'the finest of all the many ships they had given the Navy'.

The *Britannia* served as flagship to Admiral Russell (afterwards Earl of Orford) at his decisive but unappreciated victory at the Battle of Barfleur on 19 May 1692.

In 1700(?) she was rebuilt at Chatham, and again in 1719, this time at Woolwich. After serving as a hospital ship for a number of years she was eventually broken up in 1749.

Both models show the vessel as originally built in 1682 with the characteristic compartmented decoration of the period, and in the waterline version the Royal Standard is shown at the main, the Lord High Admiral's flag at the fore, a Union Jack at the spritsail topmast, a Union flag at the mizzen and the flag of the senior naval squadron, the Red Ensign at the stern.

The small craft off the port bow is a Dutch, sprit-rigged fishing vessel with her nets out.

20. HMS *St Albans* (1687)
50-gun, 4th rate, 2-decker

Admiralty Board and waterline models, scales 16′–1″ and 32′–1″, $9\frac{1}{2}″$ and $5\frac{7}{8}″$ long

The original dockyard model of the *St Albans* once belonged to the late Mr Robert Spence and I had the pleasure of seeing it at his home at Frognal in 1956, when he told me that the model was originally covered with 'black varnish'. He subsequently cleaned and restored it.

I believe the model was at one time on loan to the Science Museum as they have three good photographs of it and better still have photos of two large-scale plans

marked: 'Measured and drawn by Herbert Read, 1926.' These are the only detailed plans of a seventeenth-century dockyard model and are excellent to work from.

The *St Albans* was built by John Shish at Deptford. Her dimensions were: length on the gun deck 128′, length of keel 107′, beam 32′, and tons burden 615. Her armament consisted of twenty-two 18-pounders on the gun deck, twenty-two 9-pounders on the upper deck and probably ten 6-pounders on the quarter deck. Her complement averaged about 200 varying with peace or war establishment and foreign or home service. There is a letter to the Ordnance Department from a complaining Samuel Pepys saying, 'How it came to pass I know not . . . but the King has understood from Captain Constable that the "St Albans" has four ports on the quarter deck which the Establishment has provided no guns for.'

The *St Albans* was probably named after James Beauclerk, 1st Duke of St Albans, one of Charles II's sons by Nell Gwyn. The vessel was wrecked in 1693.

The model agrees to within six inches of the ship and shows a square tuck which is a little unusual for a vessel of this size and date. A further interesting feature of the original model is that the arms of Fisher Harding appear in the carved work at the break of the quarter-deck. It is known from the records that Harding was employed in a subordinate capacity at the Deptford yard so he probably had a good deal to do with the building of the *St Albans* and perhaps built the model himself. Harding later became one of the leading shipwrights of the time and in 1692 built the larger 3rd-rate HMS *Boyne*, the model of which, a very handsome colourful specimen with the typical open timbering of a Harding model, is at Greenwich.

The culmination of Harding's career was the construction of HMS *Royal Sovereign*, the superb 100-gun, 1st-rate, 3-decker launched at Woolwich in 1701. Unfortunately the original dockyard model of this ship was one of six models given by William III to Czar Peter the Great of Russia. These models are now rapidly deteriorating in a museum in Leningrad.

The original model of the *St Albans* is now in Trinity House, London. Mr Spence made a replica which I believe may be in the dockyard museum at Portsmouth.

As far as I know there are no contemporary pictures of the *St Albans*, even the Van de Veldes seem to have missed her, but we cannot move out of their period without a further mention of these two Dutchmen, father and son, who became marine painters to the court of Charles II. It is obvious from the number of times their name has appeared in the preceding pages how their work dominates the data sources for ship model building of this period.

Mr M. S. Robinson's magnificent *Catalogue of Drawings in the National Maritime Museum made by the Elder and the Younger Willem Van de Velde* (CUP 1958), is an ever-present aid as indeed has been Mr Robinson's personal help to me on many occasions.

Over the years I have acquired quite a considerable collection of photos of drawings, grisailles and paintings by these two remarkable artists and I fear more time than should be, is spent just browsing through them.

One could wish that the elder Willem had continued his outstanding grisaille pen paintings much more prolifically when he came to England as those he did of earlier Dutch ships must be the most detailed pictures of ships ever made. One could wish, too, that the younger Willem didn't scribble quite so often but with enough time and study one just begins to know which scribble indicates a lion and which slightly different one a unicorn.

The dockyard version of the *St Albans* is a replica of the original model but a quarter the size. The waterline version shows the vessel as the flagship of a small detachment with two anchors down in a choppy sea with her lower ports closed; she is under the command of a rear admiral of the fleet, whose flag flies at the mizzen, and he has had the royal standard put abroad in the mizzen shrouds as the signal calling the captains in his squadron to the flagship for a council of war, and their boats surround the vessel. There are four empty ports on the quarter-deck.

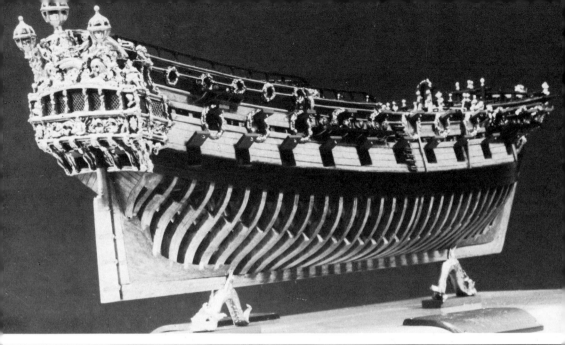
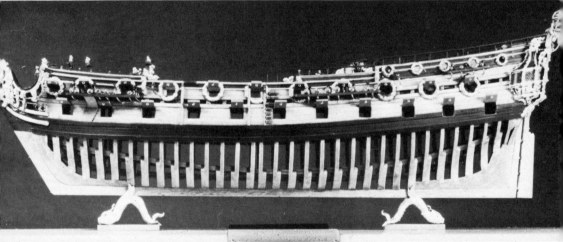

21. HMS *Lizard* (1697)

24-gun, 6th rate, single decker

Admiralty Board dockyard model, scale 16'–1", $7\frac{1}{8}''$ long

The *Lizard* was built by Robert Shortis at Sheerness. She had a gun deck length of 95', a beam of 25' and a tonnage of 264.

The original dockyard model is in the Pitt-Rivers Museum, Oxford, and was apparently donated by Dr George Clark in 1719. The model was restored and cleaned by Mr Philip Johnson in 1940.

The dimensions of the model agree reasonably well with the actual ship. One has to use the word 'reasonably' so often as some of the contemporary lists disagree with each other; also there were different ways of measuring things – keel lengths frequently being the most difficult to understand.

However the identification of the Oxford model is further confirmed by the two stands bearing the builder's initials 'R.S.' and the date ''97'. Quite a few of the dockyard models have their original stands and several have dates or initials on them. The stands themselves are usually ornate carvings of dolphins and frequently gilded.

Most of my own dockyard models have miniature versions of these stands, some incorporating appropriate badges or devices, and possibly they are some-what overdone, but the fact is that after a couple of months or so of precise, measured work on the model it is a pleasant amusement and relaxation to do something slightly flamboyant and freehand in the way of supporting mounts. The large, original models just sit in their stands by their own weight, but on miniature versions things have to be much more firmly secured by means of concealed brass rods through the keelson, floor timbers, and keel, continuing through the stand into the plinth of the glass case.

There are no pictures or plans of the *Lizard*, indeed the only piece of information I have is that she was sold on 29 July 1714 for £360.

Fortunately the authorities at the Pitt-Rivers Museum allowed us to take a great many photographs and some measurements, and with the further aid of the Keltridge drawings of 1684 and the late Mr R. J. Collins's interesting articles on a 6th-rate in the 1956 *Ships and Ship Models* some usable drawings were produced for the model.

3 THE EIGHTEENTH CENTURY

22. *Mediator* (1742)
Colonial American sloop

Waterline model, scale 16′–1″, 8¾″ long

The Colonial sloop *Mediator* was built in Chesapeake Bay and launched towards the end of 1741. Her dimensions were: length by the range of the deck 61′ 4″, length of keel for tonnage 44′, extreme breadth 21′ 2″, depth in hold 9′ 9″, burden in tons 104 74/94.

She was at first employed in the West Indies trade but in 1745 was purchased in Jamaica by the Royal Navy and immediately sent to England. Here her lines were taken off and the usual Admiralty draught produced.

She was established to mount ten carriage guns (probably 3-pounders) and eighteen swivels. The *Mediator* was subsequently employed in the Channel and was lost at Ostend late in 1745. The model was made from the draughts, which also give the spar dimensions, and shows a typical Virginia-built sloop with sharply raked mast and extremely long bowsprit and jibboom.

She is depicted as she probably appeared before purchase into the Royal Navy, that is as a West Indian trading vessel, her square topsail is being run down for furling.

I never cease to wonder at the extraordinary proportions of these Chesapeake Bay sloops. In the present example the boom projects over the stern about 19′, the bowsprit and jibboom projects from the stem by about 54′, which gives an extreme length of 140′, for a hull length of 67′ – and with her ringtail set she would have been even longer.

There are two interesting queries arising from the Admiralty draught. The first is that from experiments with this model it is impossible to use the sweep ports immediately above the channels as the deadeyes stop the sweeps being swung in an efficient manner, however these ports appear in the draught, so they must have been cut in the bulwarks of the actual ship.

The other query is the entire lack of anchor-raising apparatus on the plan. Such comparatively large anchors cannot have been brought in hand over hand, and as a vertical capstan would be unlikely, a normal horizontal windlass is shown on the foredeck, this arrangement being taken from details of other similar sloops. However, subsequent information suggests the possibility that the anchors were handled by tackles from the mast.

I am much indebted to Colonel Howard I. Chapelle of the Smithsonian Institution, Washington, for various information regarding the vessel's fittings and deck arrangements.

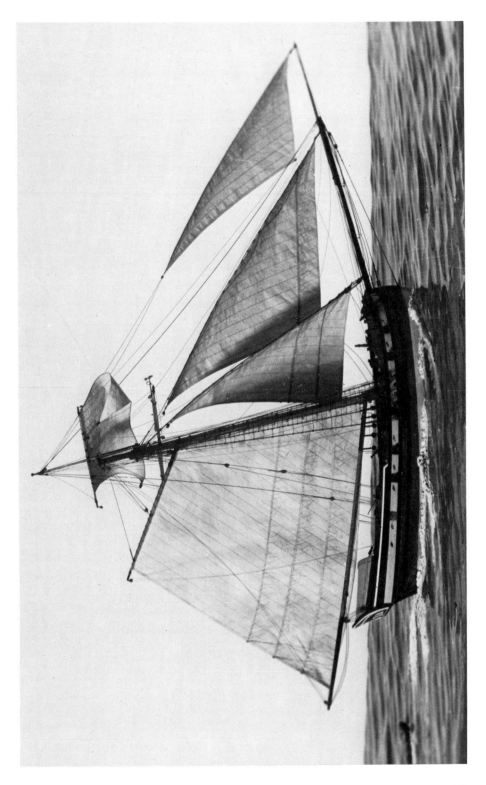

23. HMS *Medway* (1742)
60-gun, 4th rate, 2-decker

Full hull model, scale 16'–1", 14¾" long
(colour plate p. 38)

A most satisfactory subject from the research point of view as we are now into the period where the original Admiralty draughts are more often than not available from the draught room at the National Maritime Museum at Greenwich. There are three draughts of the sister ships *Medway* and *Dreadnought*, both built on the Thames to the 1733 establishment, with a gun deck length of 144', an extreme beam of 41' 5", depth of hold 16' 11" and 1068 tons burden.

Admiralty draughts are all very well of course but one needs a great deal more information for a detailed model than they give. Most fortunately, what is almost certainly the original dockyard model of the *Medway* still exists complete with original spars and rigging.

In the January 1934 issue of the old *Ships and Ship Models* there is an interesting article dealing with this model. Apparently it had been for many years in the possession of the descendants of Admiral Thomas Mathews, a Commissioner of Chatham Dockyard from 1736 to 1742. Subsequently, and quite by chance, the model was discovered in the contents of an old Welsh castle, put up for sale for probate and valued at only a few pounds. It was acquired by the Royal United Services Institution, Whitehall, and when this unusual museum was sadly disbanded the model went to Greenwich. This is a tale so satisfactory and romantic as to seem scarcely true, but apparently it is. One can only hope, even at this late hour, for further Celtic castles similarly stocked!

Thanks to the usual helpful kindness of the staff at the National Maritime Museum I was able to take many colour photos of this *Medway* model and also to take complete measurements of the masts and spars together with the sizes of many other items not shown on the draughts.

Of all the models I have built since the war the *Medway* is only the second one that has required the underwater hull being planked, all the other models have either been waterline, coppered or unplanked dockyard models. The original large model of the *Medway* is not planked below the wales, just a painted hull carved from the solid. On my own model at a quarter the size I found this area of planking most difficult to do.

On some large models one sees the hull planking scored in on the solid hull. I thoroughly disagree with the appearance of scored planking especially above the wales where it is easy enough to do properly with separate scale-width planks. However I have yet to find a way of planking lower hulls which gives a satisfactory result together with reasonable efficiency of execution.

The actual *Medway* must have been a most attractive and colourful ship. Apart from the usual red work inboard and on her gunport lids, she had both black and blue ground colours for her frieze painting and indeed there was quite a lot of blue about her, all of which shows up well her yellow mouldings and carved work.

When making the model I was requested to leave the glass cover of the case unsealed and I understand that her owner removed this and has the model mounted in a specially pierced opening in an interior party wall. With concealed, cool lighting and both sides glazed this must be quite effective and is a sensible way of getting best value for money from a model: the port side seen from the dining-room and the starboard from the drawing-room.

24. *Grosvenor* (1770)

26-gun, East Indiaman

Waterline model, scale 16′–1″, 13¾″ long

The Honourable East India Company's ship the *Grosvenor* was built by Wells of Deptford and launched in 1770. She was apparently built on the bottom of a previous *Grosvenor* of 1762.

Her dimensions were: 138′ 10″ extreme length, 111′ 10″ length of keel for tonnage, 35′ 3½″ extreme breadth, 14′ 3″ depth in hold and 741 tonnage by measurement. She was a typical East Indiaman of her period with very full underwater lines, a fairly fine run aft and the usual graceful galleried stern. Her armament consisted of twenty 9-pounders and six 6-pounder cannon. The average East Indiaman carried only two ship's boats, but the *Grosvenor* was exceptional in this respect as she was equipped with longboat, pinnace, yawl and jolly boat.

The *Grosvenor* made three complete voyages in 1771/2, 1775/6 and 1778/9. Her last fateful voyage began on 3 June 1780 and she was wrecked on 4 August 1782. The loss of the ship with her rich cargo and the subsequent misfortunes of her survivors form one of the most remarkable stories of sea disaster.

The model shows the *Grosvenor* in a fresh breeze in Eastern waters and below St Helena, the fore and main topgallant sails are being taken in and the port fore anchor is secured with a stopper and shank painter ready to let go.

Unfortunately the *Grosvenor*'s original draughts are apparently no longer in existence and, apart from a gouache by the contemporary artist George Carter, there is no picture of her. However some detailed dimensional information about the ship was obtained from the India Office Library at the Commonwealth Relations Office and some excellent draughts of the East Indiaman *Glatton*, an almost identical vessel, were obtained from Greenwich. Further data sources were the paintings of East Indiamen by Luny, Cleveley, Brooking and Serres.

Few contemporary models of East Indiamen seem to have been made but there are two very fine ones in the Rogers Collection at Annapolis and photos of these were of much assistance. Chapman's *Architectura Navalis Mercatoria* has many drawings of merchant ships of this period. These furnished further information and I was greatly helped by correspondence with Professor Percival R. Kirby of Grahamstown, South Africa, the expert on the *Grosvenor* disaster.

It was customary during the *Grosvenor* period for East Indiamen and naval vessels to anchor in St Helen's Roads, off the Isle of Wight, on their outward voyage to take in supplies of fresh water from a particularly sweet well on shore. Whilst the crew were at this task they also obtained pieces of sandstone from the fabric of St Helen's old church, and from the tombstones in the graveyard. These were brought on board and used for rubbing down the decks, hence, perhaps, the word 'holystone'.

During the construction of this particular model a visit was made to the Isle of Wight, with a brief-case concealing a large hammer and cold chisel. A small quantity of holystone was obtained from the remaining ruined tower of St Helen's old church, and a minute piece of this is shown on the port side of the

forecastle deck. We have not enquired if this constituted sacrilege, desecration or just wilful damage.

I sometimes think that ship model builders, myself included, make the decks of their models much too neat and tidy, especially if they are meant to be realistic waterline models. By contemporary reports the decks of East Indiamen must have been chock-a-block with hen coops, pigsties and cattle pens, the ship's boats loaded with bales of fodder and sometimes with the animals themselves. I don't see how one can do this without distracting attention from the actual ship, so I have to be content with a few chicken coops inside the bulwarks.

For some reason the photos of this model have been reproduced more often than those of any other model. Two pictures appear in Professor Kirby's book *The True Story of the Grosvenor East Indiaman* and a picture of the bow view forms the central motif for a series of Delft plates produced in 1960.

25. HMS *Queen Charlotte* (1790)

100-gun, 1st rate, 3-decker

Waterline model, scale 32′–1″, 9¾″ long (colour plate p. 36)

The *Queen Charlotte* was built, with her sister ship the *Royal George*, at Chatham. Her gun deck length was 190′, beam 52′ 5″, depth in hold 23′ 3″, and tonnage 2286. On the lower gun deck she carried thirty 32-pounders, on the middle deck twenty-eight 24-pounders, on the upper deck thirty 18-pounders and on the quarter deck and forecastle twelve 12-pounders.

She was Admiral Howe's flagship at the Battle of the Glorious First of June in 1794, and the famous de Loutherborg painting of this battle shows a good view of her bow and figurehead. In 1800 she accidentally caught fire and blew up killing 700 of her crew.

The *Queen Charlotte* is an excellent subject for a model. There is a complete set of draughts at Greenwich together with a fine dockyard model and there is another larger but unfinished dockyard model in the Science Museum. Both show certain differences from each other and the draughts, but this is only to be expected.

The carving and decoration on the Greenwich model is particularly well done. On the underside of the floors of the two open stern galleries there are neatly painted panels, musical instruments on the lower one and the arms of war on the upper one – delights rarely seen on this large model I suspect, and hardly possible to see on my own small waterline version. However it must have been possible to see them to advantage from a small boat coming up to the stern ladders on the actual ship.

The figurehead on the *Queen Charlotte* is a particularly fine specimen: a full-length portrait of the Queen herself with crown, orb and sceptre under an ornate umbrella-like canopy with complicated and involved supporting figures either side. There are large-scale port and starboard drawings of it included in the draughts. For these rather important figureheads I often make two simultaneously and then fit the best one; even though this is a rather complicated head it is convenient to do as the actual figure can be made off the model.

There is a very large, outdoor, waterline model of the *Queen Charlotte* at the entrance to the RN Depot at Whale Island, Portsmouth. I have a vague memory that the original figurehead used to be there also but it was not to be seen on our last visit.

The model shows the ship with an Admiral of the Fleet's Union flag at the main truck, most of her lower sails are set with the main topgallant being hoisted. Neither flying jibboom nor spritsail topsail yard is rigged.

26. HMS *Brunswick* (1790)

74-gun, 2-decker

Admiralty Board dockyard model, scale 16′–1″, 13⅛″ long
(colour plate p. 39)

The 74-gun ship was one of the most successful types of the period, armed with twenty-eight 32-pounders on the lower deck, thirty 18-pounders on the upper deck and sixteen 9-pounders on forecastle and quarter deck. The *Brunswick's* dimensions were 176′ on the lower deck, 48′ 8″ extreme beam, and 19′ 6″ depth in hold.

Like the *Queen Charlotte* she fought at the Glorious First of June and the artist Nicholas Pocock, who apparently was an eye-witness at the battle, recorded two paintings of her, one showing the stern during her engagement with *Le Vengeur* (with much too much smoke about) and a better starboard broadside view showing her after the battle. The figurehead in the latter painting shows a gentleman with a cocked hat and a tail coat, the Duke of Brunswick himself.

Mrs Mavis Chambers of Rugby, an expert on figureheads, came to my rescue here and recalled for me the tale of the figurehead having its hat shot away during the action. A deputation from the crew went to Captain Harvey, himself wounded, and begged his cocked hat which they nailed in place, so: 'The noble duke came through it like a fighter born and bred, with his hand upon his swordhilt and his hat upon his head.' One gets the feeling that battles were nice leisurely affairs in those days!

Unfortunately Carr-Laughton in his magnificent book says the figurehead was wearing highland costume, with which a cocked hat and a long tailed coat would seem inappropriate. However in order to make the most of available information, if for no other reason, the figurehead on the model wears dark tartan trews. It is only fair to add that I indulged in a good deal of correspondence to try and locate the original head, but being damaged I dare say it did not survive.

The old ways of doing dockyard models had gone out of use by this time but there are a few models with exposed deck beams and hull timbers; the latter are shown much more like the real thing on the ship with double timbers very closely spaced. The cant frames at bow and stern are also shown, these are frames which are not at right angles to the keel but which cant towards the ends of the ship in order to reduce the amount of bevel required to give a fair run to the planking.

It is of interest too, to note the increase in size of 70-gun, 2-deckers since the time of the *Resolution* of 1667.

I have a set of standardized glass-case designs for all the rates of the seventeenth century and a case for a 3rd rate of this period is nowhere near large enough for the *Brunswick*, indeed she required a size suitable for a 1st rate of, say, 120 years earlier.

Apart from the set of Admiralty draughts, I found the large folding plates in J. R. Stevens's *Old Time Ships* of especial use. These are from Steele's *Elements of Naval Architecture*, of a slightly later date and a slightly larger ship, but they afford a great deal of welcome detail.

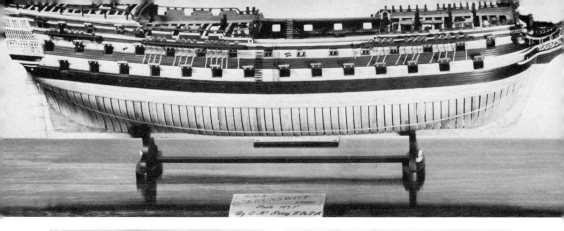

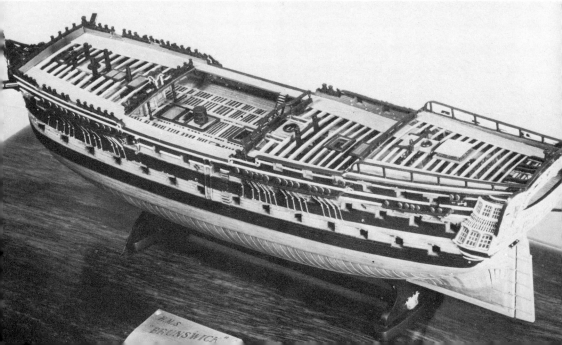

27. *Constitution* (c1798)

US frigate

Full hull and waterline models, scale 16′–1″, 18½″ long
(colour plate p. 36)

This frigate is generally regarded as America's national ship. She is still afloat and as a result of such a long life has undergone many changes, so that the problem of doing the research in order to try and produce a model showing her as she may have appeared when first in commission was considerable. With the aid of good friends the other side of the Atlantic I feel we have come reasonably near it.

To the best of my knowledge this is the first time this has been attempted and as a result of the research several slightly unusual, but well-authenticated features are shown on the model. Reference was of course made to the many previous models, and with the exception of the Salem model, few, if any of them, seem to show the ship at any precise period of her history, and the same can be said of the ship herself at Boston. Copies were obtained of all the available draughts from the original of 1796 to some dating as late as the middle of this century. All differed in one respect or another and there were even variations between the original draught and its contemporary copies.

One of the most useful sources for new information were literary ones, namely the US Government Printing Office publications entitled *Naval Documents Related to the Quasi-War with France* (1st series) and the *Naval Documents Related to the United States Wars with the Barbary Powers* (2nd series). These comprise some fourteen volumes, 400 or 500 pages each, and contain extracts from the log books of the ship, extracts from journals kept by various people aboard, and the usual official correspondence, all over the early part of the ship's life from 1797 to 1805. Short of reading the original documents these sources could scarcely be bettered. The following are some of the items resulting from all this reading.

That carronades and hammock netting were fitted in the mast tops; that she had fidded royal masts and a spritsail topsail; a spare fore topsail yard was stowed in the main chains, and on 12 October 1798 the sailmaker was making hammock cloths and waist cloths which must mean she had open bulwarks and hammock netting, and not the boarded hammock troughs she has now. This is further confirmed by Court Martial proceedings which record one of the officers habitually spewing over the netting when 'disguised in drink' on watch. Thus we see that the internal upheavals of some unsuspecting and long-dead deck officer have their uses for ship model builders in the twentieth century!

Altogether I have done six models of the *Constitution*, all to the same scale. The first five were full-hull models with furled sails and the last one was a waterline version with sails set.

The coppering of the waterline model was no great task, just a few strakes of plates along the waterline, but the full-hull models presented a very different problem, requiring between 2500 and 3000 separate plates. I see from my daily work journals that the first model took 110 hours (eleven days) to copper but by the time the fifth full-hull model had to be done some years later this time had

been very much reduced, entirely as a result of the 'increased experience, improved methods and materials' mentioned in the Introduction.

The rigging blocks were another major item. I counted some 1039 but I wouldn't swear to the exact number.

Fortunately all the work on the six models was spread over a number of years. I was able to introduce variety to a certain extent by varying the boat, anchor and spare spar stowage; on one of the models some of the guns are shown run in and the hammock netting is sometimes shown empty and uncovered and on others full and covered with the usual black painted hammock cloths, hence none of the models are at all identical.

I am much indebted to Mr Raymond Aker of Palo Alto, California, for information about the *Constitution*'s colour scheme and probable appearance in her early days.

To my mind the *Constitution* as built must have been one of the most graceful frigates of her day despite her size. The hull form given in her early draughts and her tall slender masts seem to endow her with a buoyant and elegant aspect, a quality in her I can still appreciate even though I have done too many models of her and shall do no more *Constitutions*.

4 THE NINETEENTH CENTURY

28. HMS *Euryalus* (c1805)
36-gun frigate

Waterline model, scale 32′–1″, 8″ long

There is an excellent set of plans at Greenwich for this class of frigate which includes the *Magicienne*, the *Pallas*, etc.

Actually only two of the plans are officially registered as for the *Euryalus*, but all the other sheets for the same class bear notes in contemporary hands saying: 'a copy of this drawing sent to Mr. Adams at Bucklers Hard for the building of the "Euryalus"'.

It is in instances like this that the people in the draught room at Greenwich are always so helpful in suggesting the other drawings of the same class that they have, especially appreciated when the whole matter has to be dealt with in correspondence. Lieut-Cmdr A. Waite, Mr D. J. Lyon and, until his retirement, Mr A. L. Tucker, have unvaryingly extended the greatest possible help.

There is a contemporary half-block model of the *Euryalus* and as far as I know only one contemporary picture showing her towing the *Royal Sovereign*.

As will be seen from the illustration, there is a small schooner off the frigate's port bow. This represents the famous *Pickle* that brought to England the first double-edged news of Nelson's death and the victory at Trafalgar. There seems to be little data about her of use to the ship modeller; she was built in 1803 as the *Sting*, was bought into the Royal Navy in 1805 and renamed the *Pickle*. She was wrecked off Cadiz on 27 July 1808.

I could discover no plan of her and the model is based on schooner plans of the period. Dudley Pope's *Decision at Trafalgar* gives more information about the *Pickle* than any other source that I could find, and includes the fact that she carried a spritsail yard, which seems most unusual on what must have been a very low-steeved bowsprit.

29. HMS *Victory* (c1805)
100-gun, 3-decker

Waterline model, scale 32′–1″, 10⅜″ long

There must have been more models made of Nelson's *Victory* than any other ship, and as a subject for ship modelling she seems to be just as popular in America as in her homeland. In my own modest library and files I must have references to at least two dozen models of her.

Of all those I have seen I have no doubt in naming my own two prime favourites: Wyllie's waterline model at Portsmouth and Longridge's model in the Science Museum. These two models are as different as it is possible for them to be. The Portsmouth model, showing the ship in her early condition, is a marvellously alive and colourful expression of the ship under way with movement in the sails being handled and in the most realistic sea. Seeing this model never fails to give me the greatest pleasure, but one could wish it to be better and more spaciously displayed, ideally against a plain light background.

The Science Museum model on the other hand is a full-hull version, structurally as the ship appeared in 1805. A magnificent piece of craftsmanship to start with, but also a cool classical exposition of the ship's anatomy. The coppering is well done and all the excellent boxwood-work is clearly seen, it being unpainted.

Unfortunately for many years now it has been poorly exhibited, mounted in a very third-rate model of a dry dock, quite out of harmony with the model itself.

The model builder ambitious to do the *Victory* is well catered for. He has the actual ship at Portsmouth, the draughts and the original dockyard model at Greenwich, and Dr C. Nepean Longridge's well-written and beautifully illustrated book *The Anatomy of Nelson's Ships*, which describes so well the building of his model. To top it all we have A. R. Bugler's *H.M.S. 'Victory'* – a monumental work on the ship herself so detailed as to chart the course of almost every death-watch beetle! Both books include sets of drawings.

Most model builders wish to show the ship as she appeared at Trafalgar and this is where the controversy begins. What was the sea like, how fast was she going just before the action, how many sails did she have set, were her boats stowed or towed? Just for good measure we have Dr Anderson, in his *Mariner's Mirror* review of Bugler's book, letting the cat out of the bag that the forecastle bulwarks on the ship at Portsmouth are not as they were at Trafalgar.

Probably all these queries will never be solved satisfactorily; in the event of my doing another *Victory* it would have to be a 1765 dockyard version.

The model illustrated here was made from the Longridge book, greatly aided by many photographs taken on board. The object of the exercise was to attempt to show the ship at Trafalgar a moment before she received her first damage, a shot through her main topgallant sail from the *Héros*.

The model was made sometime ago now but I did a great deal of reading to try and establish this appearance. Were I to do another now I might alter the bulwarks but nothing else.

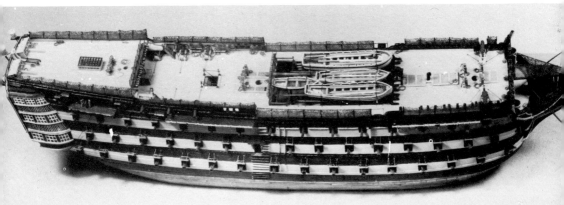

30. *Hecate* (c1818)
18-gun brig-of-war

Waterline model, scale 16'–1", 11¾" long

The *Hecate* was one of a very large class of 18-gun brigs generally known as the 'Columbine' class, a class seemingly numbered in scores, as on some of the draughts every available blank space is taken up with the usual notes to the effect that copies of the drawings were sent all over the place for one vessel or another of the senes.

The brig *Grasshopper* is included. She was captured by the Dutch in 1811 and renamed *Irene* and is the subject vessel of Mr E. W. Petrejus's book *Modelling the Brig-of-War 'Irene'*, essential reading for those wishing to build brigs and much else besides.

The *Hecate* had a 100' length on the range of the deck, an extreme beam of 30' 6" and a depth in hold of 12' 9". She was designed to carry sixteen 32-pounder carronades and two 6-pounder cannon. She was built by a Mr King at Upnor in 1809.

The *Hecate* was subsequently sold out of the Service and became the flagship of a small squadron of five vessels commanded by Thomas Cochrane, Earl of Dundonald when he sailed from Valparaiso to liberate Lima in August 1820.

She was renamed *O'Higgins* after the Director Supremo of the Chilean State, this gentleman rejoicing in the full, sonorous designation of Bernardo O'Higgins.

The model shows her under all plain sail with a red, white and blue starred pendant at the main truck and the, then, new Chilean flag at the gaff peak.

31. *Great Western* (1837)
Paddle steamer

Waterline model, scale 32′–1″, 8½″ long

The *Great Western* was the first of Brunel's remarkable trio and perhaps the best looking of the three. She was the first steamer constructed especially for the Atlantic ferry service and was quite deliberately conceived by Brunel as a further extension of his Great Western Railway.

She was particularly strongly built and well appointed. Her 75′ long saloon was stated to be the largest and most luxurious room afloat.

The *Great Western* crossed the Atlantic sixty-four times in all and also did duty on the Southampton–West Indies route. She was finally broken up at Vauxhall in 1857.

Just after the war I did the research (if such it could be called) and my wife made a model of the *Great Western* based almost entirely on the photos of the Science Museum model.

Much more recently, thanks to the good offices of Mr B. W. Bathe, of the Science Museum, a great deal more data have come to hand including a set of the original hull lines and the complete drawings for the Science Museum model which was made in 1937 presumably to celebrate the centenary of the ship's first voyage.

During the interval I had collected a number of photos of contemporary pictures of the *Great Western*, most of them quite bad. She seems to have been particularly badly served in this respect and one gains the impression that the

93

artists were used to ordinary sailing ships but the new steamship had them at a loss.

The best of the pictures were done by Joseph Walter and these differ unaccountably one from another on quite important points. Consequently a great many queries arose and I have to admit it was a much simpler and happier process building the original post-war model in ignorance. The main query was whether the *Great Western* had a forecastle deck level with the bulwarks. The large Science Museum model has no forecastle but nearly all the contemporary pictures show men walking on a deck forward at the rail level and most impressive of all, the first three sections of the body plan of the original hull lines were extended up to rail height; all the rest only to the level of the main deck. This in itself raised further difficulties too complicated to explain here, but eventually a forecastle deck was evolved with a curved after break.

So often one has to do something on a model to accommodate the seemingly conflicting information one has without any really firm basis for it – trivial problems by everyday standards perhaps, but for the serious ship model builder matters of great concern.

Confidence was not exactly inspired by one of the original drawings of the engines, having writ large upon it in a contemporary hand 'N.B. There is a more correct drawing than this.'

Mr Graham Farr in his interesting little booklet on the *Great Western* mentions two contemporary models, a simple half-model and a beautifully made builder's half model. The latter, he says, disappeared from the Seamen's Institute, Prince Street, Bristol. I can only echo his sentiments that news of its fate would be welcomed.

The model shows the ship in rather brisk conditions with reduced fore and aft canvas and a reefed topsail. Off the starboard bow is a small fishing lugger similar to those shown in the contemporary pictures.

32. *Archimedes* (1838)
Screw steamer

Full hull model, scale 16′–1″, $11\frac{1}{4}$″ long (colour plate p. 112)

One of the earliest, screw-driven steamships, designed by Henry Wimshurst for the Ship Propeller Co founded by Sir Francis Pettit Smith.

There are two good engravings of the ship, one by Rosenburg and the other by Duncan, both from paintings by Huggins. One is a straightforward port broadside view and shows clearly everything one could expect to see from such a viewpoint, especially good for the masts, spars and rigging. The other is a starboard quarter view showing the stern clearly but with the vessel heeling away from the viewer.

In the centre of the lower border of these two prints is a small, partly cut-away

sheer elevation with mast stubs and a scale of feet. Also listed are the basic dimensions of the ship.

In the Science Museum is a simple, non-detailed, carved, wooden block model of just the stern of the *Archimedes*, demonstrating the revolutionary spiral propeller.

The above is all I could find on this elusive ship. Indeed this model is a classic case of doing, for months on end, all the right things by way of research, and getting nowhere at all.

My *Archimedes* file is full of would-be helpful, but negative, letters from eight journals, four museums, four libraries, five institutes, the Public Records Office, the Patents Office, the National Register of Archives, Lloyds, etc etc.

I feel sure Wimshurst's deck plans and hull lines are tucked away somewhere together with other details, but to locate them is the problem. One good thing that did come out of this frustrating business was the knowledge that everyone approached at least wished to be helpful.

Such a notable ship, so recent and yet so little known.

33. HMS *Southampton* (c1840)
52-gun, 4th rate

Full hull model, scale 32′–1″, 10″ long (colour plate p. 107)

The building of the *Southampton* started at Deptford in March 1817 but she was not launched until 1820. Designed as a 60-gun ship she was reduced to 52 guns before completion. She was one of a series of six vessels, all the same class, built between 1817 and 1843. The others were the *Winchester, Portland, Lancaster, Worcester* and *Chichester*.

The *Southampton*'s dimensions were: length on the deck 173′ 1″, keel length for tonnage 145′ 8″, breadth extreme 43′ 8″, breadth moulded 43′, depth in hold 14′ 6″, burden in tons 1477. Armament consisted of thirty long 24-pounders on the main deck and on the quarter deck and forecastle twenty 42-pounder carronades and two long 24-pounder cannon. As was the case with the rest of the class she was again reduced to 50 guns during the late 1830s.

She was commissioned as flagship on the Cape Station in 1841, later going as flagship on the south-east coast of America. She then did various duties as a guardship and as a training ship until the summer of 1912 when she was sold for breaking up on the Tyne.

As might be expected of a ship that was a long time being built and suffered various early modifications, there are a good number of her plans at Greenwich. The earlier ones show the usual square stern and the later ones show how this was altered to the new round stern with gunports angled to give a better arc of fire.

The consequent new arrangement of quarter galleries and stern windows is not shown adequately on the plans, but at Greenwich there is a model of the stern of her sister, the *Worcester*, which shows their unusual and interesting shape rather well. She has the round bow as well, and although these features may not look as nice as the old square stern and the square beakhead bulkhead, continuing the framing and the planking right round to the centre line both ends made a much stouter ship. The square sterns and beakheads of an earlier time were of a comparatively light construction and ships so built were at great risk to raking fire.

There is a very pleasing lithograph by Dutton showing her at anchor with her upper sails hanging in their bunts and her studding-sail booms triced up.

The white band along her gunports shows how little sheer the decks had at this time. In the water she looks a very 'straight Jane' indeed.

34. *Britannia* (1840)
Cunard paddle steamer

Waterline model, scale 50′–1″, 5$\frac{7}{8}$″ long

There are four original draughts for the *Britannia* at Greenwich. They are all headed 'The Halifax Steam Vessels' and probably did duty with some variation for all the first Cunarders. One of these drawings is an excellent mast sail and rigging plan with most useful lists of dimensions.

It always gives me great satisfaction to read poor Dickens's description of the *Britannia*'s saloon which he likened to a long, narrow hearse with windows in the side, a melancholy stove at one end and long, long tables either side, and then to look at the *Britannia*'s deck plan. There is the saloon with its sash windows, a very small stove at one end just forward of the mizzen mast and two long tables, about 33′ long, either side.

But it gives me some unease to look at the official Cunard Steamship Co model in the Science Museum and find that no such long deckhouse exists on the model, indeed the deck arrangements are very unlike the ship in many ways.

The draughts show a very neat vessel with a proportionable head and not at all heavy around the quarters.

The *Britannia* was rigged as a three-masted barque and was just under 300′ long from jibboom tip to mizzen boom tip. This was considered so large that she had to be swung out into the mid-stream of the Mersey in order to take her passengers from a tender. She crossed the Atlantic forty times, was sold to the German Government in 1849 and was finally brought back to Glasgow to be broken up.

There is a contemporary print of her, icebound in Boston Harbour, in 1844 and another well-executed print giving a good starboard broadside view but bearing the names of all the early vessels, *Britannia*, *Acadia*, *Caledonia* and *Columbia* in the lower margin of the print.

The model shows the ship with all sails set except for the main course which is furled to the yard. At the foremast she flies as a complimentary flag the 1837 Stars and Stripes, and at the main the two pennants of the British and North American Royal Mail Steam Packet Co and the usual Red Ensign at the gaff peak.

35. *Great Britain* (1843)

Screw steamer

Waterline model, scale 32′–1″, 10½″ long

Brunel's second vessel, unlike the wooden *Great Western*, was built of iron plates fitted clinker-fashion to give greater strength. She was originally intended to be a paddle steamer, but as a result of the visit to Bristol by the *Archimedes* it is said that Brunel decided that the *Great Britain* should be screw propelled also.

There appear to be two sets of hull lines for the ship and a remarkably shaped mid-section they show too. There is also a series of detailed and well-drawn engravings by John Neale, published in 1847, but unfortunately these are concerned largely with the engine room area.

I have been unable to discover a deck plan apart from the rather rough sketch in the *Illustrated London News* of 15 February 1845. Little detail is shown, but what there is agrees reasonably well with the large model at the Science Museum presented to them by Thomas R. Guppy, who superintended the building of the actual ship.

There are the usual paintings and engravings of the time and the artist Joseph Walter is as much in evidence here as he was with the *Great Western*, but shows himself to be much more capable with steamships than he was then. Most authoritative of all of course is the Fox Talbot photograph taken at Bristol when she was fitting out in 1844.

The ship was altered many times during her life with various numbers of masts and funnels, none of the changes improving her original appearance.

However, over and above all this we are lucky enough to have the actual ship herself brought back from the Falklands and at the time of writing being very, very slowly restored to her original condition in Bristol. In order that this should be done with the greatest possible accuracy a remarkable amount of high-powered research has been carried out and I understand we can rely upon the prospect of her final appearance being authentic as 'convergent upon certainty'. It is to be hoped that a detailed set of plans (comparable with Campbell's restoration plans of the *Cutty Sark*) will be produced and made available when all the work is eventually finished.

The model shows the ship under power with all her sails furled. She must have been a handsome vessel, the progressive raking of her six masts being a particularly pleasing feature.

36. *Staghound* (1850)
US clipper

Waterline model, scale 32′–1″, 10″ long

This is the first of ten American clipper ships in this book and as a group these vessels of the 1850s have unique advantages from the research point of view. The most important of these, in my opinion, are the remarkable descriptions by the marine journalist, Duncan MacLean, appearing in the *Boston Atlas* and elsewhere, together with the numerous Currier engravings and I will deal with these later.

But before a series like this can be attempted it is necessary to consult the modern books which have been written on the subject.

Head and shoulders above everything else is Chapelle's *Search for Speed Under Sail* which covers very thoroughly not only this very brief golden age of American clipper building, but a great deal else besides. For the plans alone in this book we owe a considerable debt to Colonel Chapelle. Howe and Matthews *American Clipper Ships*, Cutler's *Greyhounds of the Sea*, Clark's *Clipper Ship Era*, R. McKay's *Some Famous Sailing Ships and Their Builders*, Laing's *American Sail*, Lubbock's *Colonial Clippers* and *China Clippers*, MacGregor's *Fast Sailing Ships* and last, but so far from being least as to rival Chapelle, a small booklet published in 1952, of limited edition and now a great rarity, compiled by Dr John Lyman, which gives photo-lithographic reproductions of MacLean's *Boston Atlas* descriptions of forty vessels covering the years 1851 to 1853. The *Nautical Research Journal* and *The American Neptune* also have much to offer.

I imagine there must be a good deal of most useful material in two nineteenth-century US publications, *Hall's Report on Shipbuilding* and Webb's *Plans of Wooden Vessels* . . . but good though our public lending library service is, these two books have defeated them as they appear not to be available for loan in Britain.

The *Staghound* was Donald McKay's first clipper and was built at East Boston in 1850. Chapelle gives his detailed reconstruction of her hull lines, deck plan and elevation together with contemporary description, mast and spar dimensions and original hull line drawings taken from *The Monthly Nautical Magazine*. MacLean's *Boston Atlas* article appears in Howe and Matthews and her hull lines are again reproduced in Lubbock.

I know of only one contemporary picture, of which I obtained a photograph from the Peabody Museum of Salem. This shows a port broadside of the ship under much reduced canvas and flying the two flags of the owners, Upton on the fore mast and Sampson & Tappan on the main.

The model shows her under these conditions.

37. *Nightingale* (1851)
US clipper

Waterline model, scale 32′–1″, $8\frac{3}{8}$″ long (colour plate p. 105)

The important part played by contemporary pictures in research on American clippers is well demonstrated by all four 1959 issues of *The American Neptune*. Oils, prints and photographs are generously covered by excellent pictorial supplements, these pictures so well reproduced that they may be studied under a lens with almost as much profit as an actual photographic print. A selection of these pictures are published in booklet form by the Peabody Museum.

The art connoisseur might not like American ship pictures of this period, perhaps finding them rather formal and wooden, but the ship model builder requiring detailed information could hardly ask for anything better.

The original oil paintings, many of the best by James E. Butterworth, are of interest in themselves and the engravings for the famous Currier prints taken from them seem to show even more detail.

The engravings are of course the opposite way round from the paintings and occasionally, as in the case of the clipper *Dreadnought*, show a slightly different angle, with perhaps just a little extra information for the model builder.

There can be no question at all that these artists and engravers knew about the ships they portrayed and must have done their own research either by sketching from the actual ships or the plans.

The way in which detail on the prints frequently agrees so well with the written description, the care shown in including the smaller items of rigging and showing so clearly the complicated leads of the braces, a feature that varied quite a lot from ship to ship, give me, at least, great confidence.

There are however some rather curious looking stars and stripes but I dare say these are correct too. It is just that the almost annual transmogrification of 'Old Glory' is perhaps a little too difficult for anyone in Britain!

Prints of the same picture vary greatly in quality of sharpness of detail; the Currier prints reproduced in *American Neptune*, January 1959, all come from the collection of Mrs J. Watson Webb at the Shelburne Museum, Shelburne, Vermont, and it is obvious just from the reproductions that these are some of the very best examples.

I thought it appropriate to discuss pictures of clipper ships in the *Nightingale* article as the three contemporary pictures of her expose an artistic convention, and inaccuracy, which seemed to require a very sleek-looking hull with only just the roofs of the deckhouses showing above the bulwark rails. The Chapelle elevation drawing shows bulwarks of just under 4′ high, very low for a clipper but then the *Nightingale* was quite a small vessel. The deckhouses could hardly have less than a 7′ overall height, so that from an eye-level, broadside view we have almost half the deckhouse height clearly visible above the bulwarks. This is how it is on the model and certainly how it must have been on the real ship but not in the pictures!

The *Nightingale* was built by Samuel Hanscomb Jr at Portsmouth, NH, in

Nightingale scale 32′–1″ 8⅜″ long (see opposite page)

(Opposite) *Sweepstakes*   scale 32'–1"   10¾" long   (see p. 124)

HMS *Southampton*   scale 32'–1"   10" long   (see p. 96)

(Opposite) *Great Republic*   scale 32′–1″   13¾″ long   (see p. 126)

Sir Winston Churchill   scale 16′–1″   10¼″ long   (see p. 170)

Servia   scale 50′–1″   10¾″ long   (see p. 154)

(Top) *Armadale Castle*   scale 32′–1″   18⅜″ long   (see p. 160)

(Bottom) HMY *Britannia*   scale 32′–1″   13″ long   (see p. 168)

Archimedes   scale 16′–1″   11¼″ long   (see p. 94)

U.S. CLIPPER
NIGHTINGALE
1851
Scale 32'-1"
By D.McNarry F.R.S.A.

1851 as a luxury yacht-like clipper intended to take wealthy Americans to the Great Exhibition in London in that year. Her hull lines appear in Chapelle and are also reproduced, together with a small sail plan in MacGregor. There is some brief description of her in Howe and Matthews including a rather unsatisfactory and inadequate list of spar dimensions. The *Boston Atlas* seems to have no mention of her other than a notice of auction sale which yielded the valuable information that she had a half poop deck 60′ long.

Of the three pictures mentioned, one is a Chinese oil giving a starboard broadside view and the other two are both Currier prints, showing her at anchor off The Battery, New York, one with all sails furled, the other exactly the same, still with anchor down but with all three topsails and one headsail set. Here she is obviously in the act of demonstrating to any admiring watcher on shore the quick, seaman-like technique of dropping and sheeting home her three topsails simultaneously from previously raised and trimmed yards. It must have been quite spectacular when smoothly done and even more so if the anchor fouled!

The model shows her successfully, we hope, accomplishing this manoeuvre.

38. *Witch of the Wave* (1851)
US clipper

Waterline model, scale 32′–1″, 9¼″ long

Duncan MacLean was a seaman in his earlier years who subsequently turned marine journalist. I wonder myself if he did not have some practical connection with shipbuilding as his knowledge of the structure of the clippers is quite considerable. I know of no equal to MacLean's reviews of the new tonnage of his day.

With enthusiasm and method he describes his ships, noting the quality of the workmanship, the colouring and the paintwork, with detailed descriptions of figureheads and stern decorations. On deck he deals with most of the fittings after giving enough dimensions, mast-centres, deckhouse sizes, etc, to enable a deck plan to be drawn with fair accuracy. Towards the end of his articles there is usually a nice long list of mast and spar dimensions frequently going on to some description of rigging and sails. The ship model builder's journalist if ever there was one!

MacLean also gives a great deal of information about the interior appointments of the ship, perhaps of no practical value to the ship model builder but it is pleasant to know about such delights as the following from his *Witch* description:

'This cabin is wainscotted and grained, and forms an anti-room to that abaft it, which is the great cabin. Here is splendor. Gothic panels of bird's eye maple, with frames of satinwood, relieved with zebra mahogany and rose wood, enameled cornices edged with gold, and dark pilasters, with curiously carved and gilded capitals and dark imitation marble pedestals.

Abaft of it is another cabin finished in the same style, and having three panels of mirrors forward, and another mirror aft in the rudder casing. The transom is fitted as a semi-circular sofa, covered with rich velvet.'

Of another vessel he says: 'The divan, like the transom, is covered with crimson damask and would charm the heart of an Oriental to look at it.'

Who could be bothered with a plastic-lined, first-class suite on the *QE 2* after that?

But MacLean doesn't spend all his time on cushioned sofas, he goes down into the hold and measures the rock-elm keelson; he measures and counts the hanging knees and how many spikes there are in each. Altogether from his writing one gains a remarkable impression of the vast amount of massive timbers that went into these ships – their bows, for instance, must have been virtually solid timber for quite a distance from the stem. All this stout woodwork, admirable though it was, must have reduced the cargo space.

The *Witch of the Wave* was built by George Raynes at Portsmouth, NH, in 1851. Chapelle gives her complete hull lines and plan, together with masts and spar dimensions; her lines appear again in Cutler and the MacLean description appears in Lyman.

There seem to be only two pictures of the *Witch*: an oil painting at the Peabody and a not very useful woodcut reproduced in Chapelle.

The model follows neither in setting, but shows the ship at anchor in a calm sea with accommodation ladder down and two of her boats in the water.

39. *Challenge* (1851)
US clipper

Waterline model, scale 32′–1″, 11″ long

Built by William H. Webb at New York, the *Challenge* is possibly my favourite among the American clippers I have done so far, perhaps because of the marked taper of her sail plan. MacLean mentions this in particular in his description of the vessel and there is, I believe, a general tradition that the leeches on the sails of US clippers almost always tapered in a long straight line from the clew of the course to the skysail earring. What few contemporary sail plans exist bear this out fairly well and invariably when one draws the mast and spar plan this seems to be so.

One of the most satisfying things about building these clippers is that one starts with just a list of figures, and when these are eventually translated to the masts and yards on paper, a line can be ruled from the skysail yardarm shoulder to that on the lower yard, and if all measurements are correct and the yards at their appropriate heights, this line intersects all the intervening shoulders.

The *Challenge* had her rig altered several times but I have used the MacLean dimensions.

Chapelle's plans of the *Challenge* are the most detailed of a clipper ship in his

book, and with all that extra information a pleasure to work from.

Cutler also gives the lines drawing and a sail plan, and the long and useful MacLean article appears in Lyman.

I know of five contemporary pictures of the *Challenge*: the Pearl River painting by Huqua, a lee side view for a change with plenty of rigging and flags; an excellent picture in David MacGregor's collection and reproduced in his book *The China Bird*, a woodcut of her being launched, of no great use; a Currier print, unusually enough a rather bad one; and finally a further print originally drawn by E. Brown and printed by Endicott & Co of New York. The latter is probably the most detailed and certainly shows the narrowing sail plan to perfection.

The model portrays the ship under all plain sail with N. L. & G. Griswold's blue-and-white-diced house flag at the main.

40. *Flying Fish* (1851)
US clipper

Waterline model, scale 32′–1″, 9¼″ long

Another of Donald McKay's clippers built at East Boston.

Fellow members of the Nautical Research Guild of America will remember that as a result of a great deal of research by many people in the Guild, a modern set of drawings was produced of this ship. These plans were based on a hull lines drawing in the Bergen Museum and on the MacLean description. I used these modern drawings for the model but took my mast and spar dimensions direct from MacLean's article.

There has recently been some improvement in the quality and quantity of commercial plans for ship model builders and, as we are dealing with American clippers, I must mention the very detailed plans of the *Comet* (1851) and the *Young America* (1853) produced by Crothers & Hornsby and available from P. Coker at Charleston, SC, all members of the Guild. I believe there are more to come from this stable.

However one has to make the point that there is only one way of finding out if a modern plan is any good or not and that is to build a model from it.

Just looking at it and noting that it seems to give a lot of detail is not good enough. I have yet to work from a commercial plan that is not adrift somewhere. One of the most frequent errors is that mast caps as well as mast tops are shown parallel to the waterline, but I know of no contemporary authority that shows caps other than at right angles to the mast. A small point perhaps but indicative of the kind of errors one comes across.

In some of the MacLean descriptions we have mention of specific patent fittings like Emerson's Corresponding Ventilators, John Crane's Superior Self-acting Chain Stoppers, New York Patent Pumps and the less specific but no less fascinating 'beautiful capstans made of locust and mahogany, with composition circles and pauls and brass drumheads'.

I have never been able to discover contemporary drawings of these items, and even in a general way there seems to be little known about the appearance of fittings like this in American shipbuilding for this period. I imagine ships' chandlers must have produced illustrated catalogues at this time, and in rare optimistic moments I like to think that there is perhaps a trunk full of them in an undisturbed attic in some well-preserved Victorian house in the most exclusive part of Boston, Massachusetts. I for one would certainly like to hear of any such discovery.

As far as I know there are only two contemporary pictures of the *Flying Fish*: one a painting showing a port broadside/bow view, and the other a print of the starboard side under reduced canvas. Neither is very helpful, but in R. McKay's *Some Famous Sailing Ships* . . . there is a reproduction of a very nice looking painting by Fred. S. Cozzens (not contemporary with the ship I think) showing the *Flying Fish* hove to with her main topsail aback and this model shows her in this situation.

41. *Flying Cloud* (1851)
US clipper

Full hull model, scale 16′–1″, 18½″ long

Yet another McKay production from his East Boston yard. I have the impression that this ship is the most frequently modelled of all the clippers of the 1850s.

Dr John Lyman has written a most interesting article about her in the autumn 1972 issue of the *Nautical Research Journal*, which includes MacLean's description and a very clear reproduction of the original lines plan from Henry Hall's *Report* . . . Many years ago articles on constructing a model of the *Flying Cloud* appeared in the *Popular Mechanics Magazine* and these were later made into a booklet. Reconstruction plans also appear in Magoun's *The Frigate 'Constitution' and other Historic Ships*.

There are a couple of not very useful contemporary pictures of her launching and loading, but there is one good Currier print showing a starboard broadside, lee view with weather stuns'ls set. This is a full-hull model with bare yards braced up square athwartship. I would call this the normal sort of clipper ship model, and if we leave aside the work involved in cutting and fitting between two and three thousand copper plates on the underwater hull, certainly the simplest.

Most models in this style have as little running rigging as possible, but despite the bare yards, I have fitted all the running rigging that can be justified on this particular example. Even so it is a great deal easier to do than most realistic waterline models.

Such models as the *Staghound*, *Flying Fish* and *Sweepstakes* shown in these pages pose problems to the model builder which require no small amount of imagination to solve. Braced-up yards, reefed and furling sails, the inclusion of stuns'ls and sails set aback all raise curious problems of rigging very difficult to explain and probably undreamt of by the builder of ordinary models with no sails and squared yards. There is little to be found of use in this respect in the text-books of the period and sadly there are no real clipper ship sailors left to tell us just what did happen.

The most difficult area is of course between the main and mizzen masts where the main braces go aft and the mizzen braces, sometimes crossed port to starboard, go forward, and on waterline models under sail the main gaff and the upper mizzen staysails and their rigging all have to be worked in as well, without any ropes fouling each other.

In the final analysis I suppose it all boils down to a correct visualization of what happens to various ropes when sails shown furled on the model are set and vice versa. One has a landlubber's hope that were some old sailor able to come back and see it he would find all reasonably shipshape and Bristol fashion.

42. *Sovereign of the Seas* (1852)
US clipper

Waterline model, scale 32′–1″, 9¾″ long

Generally reckoned to be one of the fastest and most handsome of the McKay clippers, in view of her fame it is amazing that there is such a divergence in the data regarding her dimensions.

Duncan MacLean, Lubbock and the figures given on the Currier print all agree, yet Colonel Chapelle's drawing in *Search for Speed Under Sail*, based on the Clark Collection drawing, is something like 20′ shorter. And just to add interest, Cutler shows a photo of the builder's original model which he says is too short as the vessel was lengthened by several frames amidships, after the model was made. He also gives a hull lines drawing, taken he says from the original model but lengthened to conform to the ship as built. Unfortunately most of his drawings lack a scale of feet.

The profile drawing of the *Sovereign of the Seas* shows to good effect the difference between the bows and sterns of British and American vessels.

McKay's bows were just about as plain and bare as they could be with only a carved figure on the stem and sometimes a little carving down to the hawseholes. Indeed I believe he even went to the extent of taking rigging in through holes in the bows and setting it up inboard so as to have as little gear as possible at the head. Altogether a very modern effect, especially as twenty years later British clippers still carried a full assemblage of trail boards, head rails, brackets, etc.

The sterns of American vessels also have a great difference, being so short and stubby in profile compared to their British counterparts, where the counters overhang the stern post a good deal more.

I always get the impression of great modernity from American hulls while their spars, sails and rigging appear very old-fashioned and man-of-war-like, but all the better looking for that.

There would seem to be only three contemporary pictures of the *Sovereign*: the well-known oil painting and the Currier print both port side lee views and frequently reproduced, and the slightly less-known engraving from the *Illustrated London News* of May 1859. The model shows her as in the Currier print but with McKay's own flag at the main.

43. *Sweepstakes* (1853)
US clipper

Waterline model, scale 32′–1″, 10¾″ long (colour plate p. 106)

Designed by Daniel Westervelt and built by his father Aaron of New York.

Chapelle gives the usual hull lines, profile and deck plan together with a list of mast and spar dimensions. A similar list, but more accurately printed, appears in *The Ship Model Builder's Assistant* by Charles G. Davis. These lists are unusual in that they include some stuns'l boom lengths. It is not stated whether they are for main or fore, but they are remarkably long by normal proportions even for main yards and give a considerable spread of canvas.

Indeed the *Sweepstakes* is quite a ship, with tall well-raked masts and long jibboom and flying jibboom in two spars.

The Currier print from a Butterworth painting is a very lively portrait and shows her to be just this. The Chambers & Heiser house flag has a unique shape.

Our oft-quoted friend Duncan MacLean invariably gives the impression that all the ships he reviews were superbly built. Friendly with the builders and parochially prejudiced as he may have been, I have little doubt in my own mind that this brief period on the east coast of America did produce some of the finest quality vessels ever built. One cannot quite believe him when he says, 'she is finished as smooth as glass'; but when he says 'Her sides are smooth as cabinet work, and every line and moulding is graduated to correspond with her sheer. End or broadside on, her appearance is truly beautiful; if cast in a mould she could not have been more perfect to the eye . . . her bulwark boarding is neatly tongued and grooved and finished in the first style of workmanship' – then one believes but wishes to confirm.

The period is a little too early for much in the way of photographs but there are two exceedingly good photos taken rather later, in 1869, of Donald McKay's last clipper the *Glory of the Seas*. They are both frequently reproduced pictures and appear in *The American Neptune* of April 1959. One can spend some time with a good lens and take great pleasure in observing the incredible evenness of the planking seams and the way in which the planks graduate to a greater width at the wales.

The much narrower planking of the bulwarks – this must be the tongued and grooved work referred to – is done even more neatly. The various rail mouldings on the hull, fancy, main and sheer, and on the edges of the channels are not just simple half-rounds but more complicated and elegant and the raised carving on the stem and trail boards is done cleanly and with restraint.

Having seen this in the photographs one would like to attempt some sort of comparison with what still exists today of this period. There is of course only the *Cutty Sark* at Greenwich, of the same date as the *Glory of the Seas*, and one can only hope that it is the ravages of time that have caused the difference!

44. *Great Republic* (1853)
US clipper

Waterline model, scale 32′–1″, 13¾″ long (colour plate p. 109)

At the time of her building, the *Great Republic* was the largest sailing ship afloat and was certainly the most ambitious of the clippers built by Donald McKay and he built her to run on his own account.

Strangely enough no review of her appears in the *Boston Atlas*, but a much longer description than usual appeared as a separate booklet complete with a set of plans and it is generally assumed that Duncan MacLean was the author as it certainly bears his stamp. I understand this booklet is a very rare item indeed but I was fortunate enough to be loaned one whilst building the model.

The plans mentioned are virtually the same as those appearing in the *Souvenirs de Marine* by Edmond Paris (1882–1908). If these plans are really McKay's own drawings then they are not as workable and consistent as one might expect, especially the spar plan which shows no mizzen skysail and is wrong elsewhere.

Also in the Admiral Paris volume is a reproduction of an excellent painting by François Roux done in 1882 giving two views of the ship as she would have looked had she ever gone to sea as built. One has the impression that this painting must have been done from the plans, but if they were, Roux corrected the mizzen by adding the skysail. The Butterworth painting and the Currier lithograph done from it both omit this item.

However, I find myself relying on MacLean's written description and his comprehensive list of mast and spar dimensions which give uncompromisingly a mizzen skysail mast and yard. Indeed from these lists of figures alone one cannot help getting a very satisfactory spar plan with the leeches of the sails tapering upwards just as they should.

MacLean gives her tonnage as 4000, length 325′ and beam 53′. She had four complete decks, or one could say her forecastle and poop were continuous, and she was coppered up to 25′ draught.

The figurehead was a large eagle's head, still extant I believe, and across her stern was a huge, gilded spread eagle spanning 36′ between wingtips.

She was rigged as a four-masted barque, her 44″-diameter mainmast and 120′-long main yard must have been the largest ever made.

The appalling disaster by fire which overtook the ship whilst loading cargo for her maiden voyage has been told often enough. The result nearly ruined McKay and the ship herself lacked her previous magnificence when rebuilt.

Captain E. Armitage McCann, an early American writer on ship model building matters, wrote a most interesting series of articles on building the *Great Republic* in the 1935/6 *Popular Science Monthly*. He wrote many other articles as well which must have started many people on a pleasurable hobby. Perhaps some of his data and methods might not stand up to today's standards but he was the leading figure of his time in this field.

The model shown here is depicted under all plain sail and in the same conditions and on the same tack as the Roux painting.

45. *Lightning* (1854)
US clipper

Full hull model, scale 16′–1″, 20¾″ long

This is the last of the US clippers in these pages and again a McKay creation. She is perhaps the least attractive to my eye as her extra-wide rig tends to give her a slightly squat appearance. Like the *Challenge* she was coppered in England.

Chapelle gives a well-detailed drawing and a sketch spar plan. He also reproduces a good deal from the US *Nautical Magazine & Naval Journal* in his appendix. Howe and Matthews reprint the MacLean article but before I started the model I was lucky enough to obtain a photostat copy of the *Boston Atlas* page with this article, and the Howe and Matthews version is inaccurate on more than one occasion.

I have one or two photos of contemporary pictures of the *Lightning* and there are very many modern paintings of her; most are misleading and some are just nonsense. However this model did introduce me, via photographs from America and Australia, to the work of the Australian artist, the late Mr D. M. Little. He did a painting of the ship entitled 'Ship "Lightning" swung to the tide, Port Phillip Head 1854'. This is such a remarkable piece of work that it was quite sometime before an American colleague and myself could believe it was not a photograph. As a ship model builder I can never give higher praise to a painting than this.

As this is the end of this group of American clippers I must express my appreciation of the kind help in research that I have received from their country of origin. Most especially to my old friend and colleague H. T. Fitzpatrick of Alabama and to Mr William Avery Baker, Colonel Chapelle and Dr John Lyman, together with many American museums, and I should add not only for the foregoing models, but also for the future American clippers I hope to build.

46. HMS *Birkenhead* (1852)
Paddle troopship

Waterline model, scale 32′–1″, 9¼″ long

HMS *Birkenhead* was the first iron steam vessel to be launched for the Royal Navy. Her dimensions were: length bp 210′, hull beam 37′, displacement tonnage 1918. She was built by John Laird of Birkenhead in 1845. As designed she was a particularly handsome looking ship with a clipper stem, flush deck and two masts, the foremast being square rigged. Unfortunately the Admiralty made a number of alterations to John Laird's original design. The first of these was to move the paddle shaft forward by several feet, which caused the vessel to trim by the head.

About this time the Admiralty was concerned with the relative effect of shot on the hulls of iron and wooden vessels, and an experiment was carried out by firing at the small, lightly built iron ferry boat *Ruby*.

It was later reported in evidence before a Committee of the House of Commons that the iron of which she was built was originally very thin, 'no thicker than a half crown', and that she was in a particularly bad state of repair. Needless to say the experiment had disastrous effects on the *Ruby* which were in no way comparable to the effect gunshot might have had on the very stoutly built iron hull of the *Birkenhead*.

Despite this however, the Admiralty decided to convert the vessel into a troopship and a forecastle and poop were added to the hull. This brought the vessel down in the water a further two feet, a particularly unfortunate matter for a paddle vessel. All her masts and spars were considerably reduced in size, the mainmast being moved forward two or three feet and a small mizzen stepped through the poop deck. Her original main armament of large bow and stern pivot guns were removed but she apparently kept her six 32-pounder, 25-cwt carronades.

In her new guise as a troopship she did some quite fast runs to Halifax and to Cape Town. Her final voyage in January and February of 1852 was with troops from Queenstown to South Africa. She landed some of her troops at Simonstown and was then ordered on round the Cape. On the night of 26 February 1852 she struck a rock off Danger Point, broke her back and went down quite quickly.

There were 638 souls on board at the time and 454 of them were drowned, all the women and children being saved. The remarkable steadiness of the troops during this disaster won world renown even to the extent of the King of Prussia causing an account of their behaviour to be read to every regiment in his army.

The Admiralty draughts of the period are particularly well drawn and contain a mass of detail and there are quite a number of drawings of the *Birkenhead*, the upper deck plan and one of the profile draughts being particularly complicated. I remember when building the model wondering if I would ever get to the masts and rigging, and Parkinson's Law certainly raised its ugly head. Her considerable alterations are shown on the original draughts in the form of numerous ticks, crosses and adjustments in different coloured inks and it requires some

patience to sort this out on an entirely black and white photostat.

It is interesting to note that as well as hammock troughs around her bulwarks, she has numerous hammock racks on her deck and a large circular one encompassing the base of her funnel – presumably this extra hammock accommodation was required for the troops she carried. She is also fitted with an early type of cowl ventilator, which I call the 'bandaged' type as the cowl part is made from overlapping strips of metal.

But perhaps her most interesting feature is the two large metal lifeboats stowed upside down to cover large openings in the tops of her paddle boxes. By an ingenious arrangement of davits and tackles the boats can be raised, righted and lowered into the water; similar equipment is described and illustrated in Peake's *Rudimentary Treatise on Shipbuilding* (c1850).

The *Birkenhead* is shown here during her last voyage at anchor with her sails loosed and drying. She flies the commander's pennant at the main and the Red Ensign at the mizzen gaff peak.

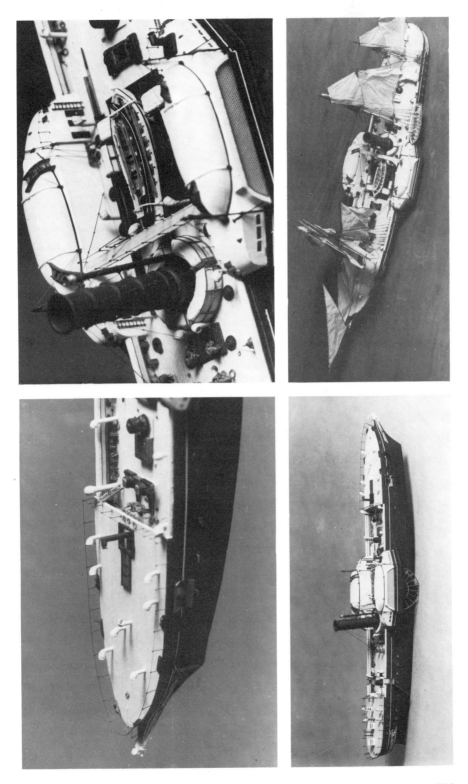

47. *Scotia* (1861)
Cunard paddle steamer

Waterline model, scale 50′–1″, 8¾″ long

The last Cunard paddle steamer and probably the most handsome paddle vessel ever built. She was very strongly made of iron, had an overall length of 400′, a beam of 47′ 10″ and drew 20′ of water. Her paddle wheels, which had fixed radial floats, were 40′ in diameter and she was brig rigged. She served on the North Atlantic route for about thirteen years and held the Blue Riband for five of them.

She is a most satisfactory subject for a ship model as she not only looks well but the research requires only reasonable effort since the original builder's model is in the Science Museum at South Kensington where I was allowed to take a number of close-up photos. Moreover there are two very detailed plates of plans in John Scott Russell's *The Modern System of Naval Architecture* (1864) which give hull lines, inboard and outboard profiles and the plans of three decks. Another plate of drawings, whose origin I am not absolutely sure of but I believe may be from Reed's *Shipbuilding in Iron and Steel* (1868), shows six transverse sections and one longitudinal section. There is also a Currier and Ives print of a starboard broadside view.

The *Scotia* has symmetrical paddle-box facings, the curve being the same forward as aft, so it is most convenient to be able to cast two identical carved facings from the same mould. Many paddle-boxes have a different curve down to the sponson at their after end, and I always think it is one of the numerous minor injustices of life that two opposite handed castings cannot be got from the same mould!

48. CSS *Alabama* (1862)
Confederate States raider

Full hull model, scale 32′–1″, 8¾″ long

As a British subject as often as not making models of American ships for American citizens I feel I should steer a very exact course along the Mason-Dixon Line. As the reader will have just gone through no less than ten Yankee clippers in a row he will realize how much the steering has yawed to starboard – a deviation being currently redressed by a series of Confederate blockade runners.

However, despite all this, I am bound to admit to a most partisan feeling where the *Alabama* is concerned.

On 15 June 1862 a sleek dark vessel, No 290, was making her trial run down the Mersey having just recently left the ways of John Laird of Birkenhead. She was a wooden corvette of fairly light scantling with a coppered lower hull, three masts with yards on fore and main and a single left-handed, retractable brass propeller. Her length between perpendiculars was 214′, her moulded breadth 32′, her gross tonnage 682, and she cost £51,716.

Due to intrigue and speculation surrounding her building and her ultimate ownership, great secrecy was observed at her place of building. Eventually she got up steam and sailed off, again ostensibly for another trial run along the English coast. Once at sea however, the notable ladies and gentlemen on board for this occasion were promptly transferred to an accompanying tender and No 290 proceeded to the Azores where she was coaled, munitioned and armed with six 32-pounder broadside carriage guns, one 8″ smooth-bore pivot and one 100-pounder Blakely rifled gun.

Amid some ceremony the Stars and Bars was broken at her mizzen peak and she was named *Alabama* of the Navy of the Southern Confederate States of America.

From then on she proved a phantom-like menace to the merchant ships of the Northern Federal States, capturing, burning and sinking at such a remarkable rate that the Federal ships were almost driven from the seas.

One of these episodes, the capture of the Boston vessel *Sea Bride*, took place off Cape Town, the proceedings being watched by thousands from the vantage points of Lion's Hill and Kloof Road.

Having no home port where she could refurbish with leisure and safety, the *Alabama* was kept at sea constantly for two years, by which time her boilers needed attention, her copper was foul and curling and worst of all the powder in the percussion caps of her shells had gone dull.

It was in this state that she sailed out of Cherbourg Harbour one bright Sunday morning in June 1864 to meet the chain-clad Federal sloop-of-war *Kearsage*. Once free of the three-mile limit a fierce and circling battle commenced, once again watched by spectators on the shore, and from various contemporary reports of the conflict the *Alabama* might well have been the victor had it not been for the shortcomings of her powder.

During the fight one of her shells lodged in the sternpost of the *Kearsage*. Had

it exploded as it should, the Northern vessel would have been unable to manoeuvre. (The sternpost was later sawn out complete with shell and preserved by order of President Lincoln.) As it was, the battle continued until the *Kearsage*'s superior weight of metal eventually told and the *Alabama* was put out of action, lowering her flag as she sank by the stern.

Whatever the ethics of *Alabama*'s ruthless raiding activities on unarmed merchant vessels, it cannot be denied that she had a truly amazing career which was very aptly summed up in an issue of the London *Times* in 1864: '. . . this quick and cunning craft that raced so swiftly and roamed the deep so long. She was a good ship, well handled and well fought, and to a nation of sailors that means a great deal. So ends the log of the "Alabama" – a vessel of which it may be said that nothing in her whole career became her like its close!'

The model is in the full hull style of the builder's model of the 1860s and shows the complete underwater hull covered with over 2000 copper plates. The port broadside guns are shown run in for loading and the starboard run out for firing, the big pivot guns stowed on the centre line. The sails are unbent and the yards lowered harbour-fashion.

The 1861, 7-star Confederate ensign is at the mizzen gaff peak and the commander's pennant at the main truck. It is of interest to note that in the August 1973 issue of the *Mariner's Mirror* an item appeared regarding the *Alabama*'s flag, rescued after the battle and still in existence. It is described as being a large white flag, the top corner next to the flagstaff being red with a St Andrew's Cross of blue imposed on it. On the cross are thirteen white stars representing the original thirteen United States. Somewhat different from the generally accepted design!

The model is based on the builder's original large-scale model still preserved at Birkenhead, on various photographs, prints and paintings of the ship and on contemporary written accounts by her captain, Raphael Semmes and her first officer, John McIntosh Kell.

I am especially indebted for various information to Cammell Lairds of Birkenhead, Mr E. W. Paget-Tomlinson one-time keeper of shipping at Liverpool Museum, Mr Ian Calder late of Warrington, Lancashire, and most especially to Mr H. T. Fitzpatrick of Montgomery, Alabama, whose own 16'–1" waterline version of the ship is the undoubted definitive model of the *Alabama*.

49. *Great Eastern* (c1865)
Screw/paddle steamer

Waterline model, scale 32′–1″, 22″ long

Built of iron and launched at Millwall in 1858 this quite extraordinary vessel had a length on the waterline of 680′, a hull beam of 82·7′ and a displacement tonnage of 32,000. She was the joint product of Isambard Kingdom Brunel and John Scott Russell and was the largest vessel ever built for nearly fifty years.

Her enormous proportions – five funnels, six masts, 56′-diameter paddle wheels and 24′-diameter screw (the latter the largest ever made) – give her an unique place in naval architecture. Being so much before her time was perhaps partly the reason for her failure as a passenger ship. Her most useful work was done between 1865 and 1873 when she laid a number of submarine telegraph cables. The model shows her laying her first, unsuccessful Atlantic cable in 1865, and in fitting her out for this task it was necessary to remove her No 4 funnel and boilers to make room for one of the cable tanks.

Unlike the *Scotia*, the *Great Eastern* could hardly be recommended as the subject for a model; even to attempt to show her as originally built would be difficult enough.

There is a lot of material available on the *Great Eastern* – the plans from Russell's work and also some special 'picture plans' he presented to the Science Museum together with his large model also at the museum – but all of these vary one from another so much that it is impossible to know what is right. Most of the early photos are of poor quality and rarely datable.

However it doesn't start to get really difficult until one is asked to do the *Great Eastern* as she appeared on a particular voyage as a cable layer. I am sure there must still exist more useful information about this voyage than I was able to find after pretty well a year's research.

Rolt's *I. K. Brunel*, Dugan's *The Great Iron Ship* and Clarke's *Voice Across the Sea* all supplied general data but most useful of all was Sir William H. Russell's book *The Atlantic Telegraph*. Russell was the correspondent of the London *Times*. He went on the 1865 voyage and fortunately had with him the artist Robert Rudley. The text of the book must come from Russell's newspaper reports and its excellent engravings from Dudley's paintings.

The great problem of course is the complicated 'picking-up' and 'paying-out' machinery. Probably nothing like it had ever been made before so there was no other source to draw from. Russell gives amazingly complicated descriptions of the cable's path from hold to stern wheel. Dudley's pictures of the machinery are equally remarkable (and sometimes incomprehensible) and the model could not have been done without them. However there were many small queries very difficult to resolve.

Dudley's pictures also give a good idea of the life on board during this voyage, often with too many human figures hiding useful detail. Nevertheless there are good ideas for slightly unusual things on the model: there are several windsails which I had not previously done, a hatch canvas cover is shown thrown back,

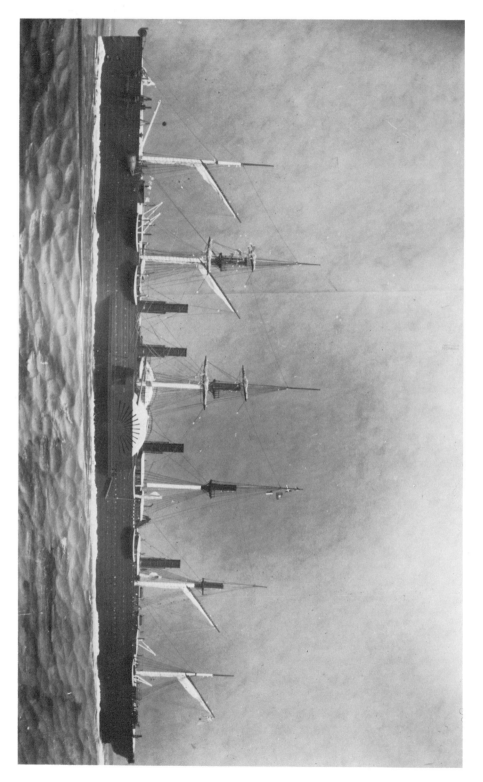

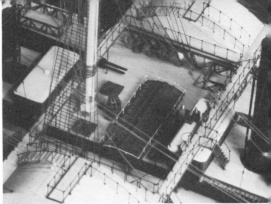

there is a line of washing (the garments scaled to my own size) a saw horse with a saw and some odd planks of wood.

The artist depicts a hoist of signal flags on the fourth mast but I was unable to read them in his picture so, as has happened many times, the flag expert, Alec Purves, came to the rescue and suggested a four-flag hoist from Marryat's Code, still being used in 1865; '6480, What do you think of the weather?'

It is a matter of some curiosity that on the deck plan in Scott Russell's work the first two funnels are round and the three after ones oval, and bad though the contemporary photos are, it does seem to have been so, and I have done round and oval funnels on the model but I would very much like to know the reason for this design.

50. *Taeping* (1863)
Clipper

Waterline models, scales 32′ and 64′–1″, 8½″ and 4¼″ long respectively

The first of six British clipper ships in these pages and except for the *Cutty Sark* I am sorry to say that from the research point of view we have to work on a very different basis from that of the US clippers of a decade earlier. We lack a MacLean and the contemporary prints are less in quantity and poorer in quality. One might expect rather more and better photographs, in view of the later date, but most of those I know of are not good and make it hard enough to identify a particular ship let alone obtain detail. I fear these next few models may well turn into a saga of complaint!

From the fact that I have done three models of the *Taeping* it might be thought that there is a good deal of information, but this is not really so.

I have a hull lines plan taken off the model (presumably builder's or contemporary) in the Clark collection at the MIT, USA, by M. Costagliola in 1949, two Dutton lithographs, the ILN engraving and the brief description in MacGregor's *The Tea Clippers*.

Taeping was the first composite tea clipper built by Robert Steele of Greenock. She was 183′ 7″ long and had a beam of 31′ 1″. She was fitted with Cunningham's self-reefing topsails on all three masts.

The larger of the two models is shown under all plain sail and the smaller 64′–1″ version under furled royals and her skysail yard taken in.

51. *Ariel* (1865)
Clipper

Waterline models, scales 32′ and 64′–1″, 8½″ and 4¼″ long respectively

There are somewhat better data regarding the *Ariel*. Hull lines, deck plan, inboard works profile, rigging and sail plans have all been reconstructed and published by D. MacGregor in *The Tea Clippers, Fast Sailing Ships* and in the May 1966 issue of *Ships Monthly*.

Lubbock in *The China Clippers* reprints an interesting description of the ship by her captain and also gives an abstract of his journal during the 1866 voyage and this is of much more use than most such items.

Both these authors print a list of mast and spar measurements.

This period produced some remarkably famous ships and the *Ariel* with her almost delicate and yacht-like appearance seems a great favourite with everyone, yet most of the information we have consists of boring lists of passages, abstracts of logs, page after page of these giving only position, distance run and wind force, columns of coefficients, etc. Very unsatisfactory for the poor model builder who only wants simple answers to simple questions like what colour the yards were painted or how big was the main hatch, and not finding them can at best only make conjectural models of these beautiful and indeed recent vessels.

The larger cased model in the illustration shows the *Ariel* as she appears in the famous Dutton lithograph of the 1866 tea race and the smaller model is under plain sail.

52. *Sir Lancelot* (1865)
Clipper

Waterline models, scales 16′ and 32′–1″, 17″ and 8½″ long respectively

The hull lines of both the *Sir Lancelot* and the *Ariel* were apparently identical. There were some obvious differences in the rig, but we have the usual unsatisfactory situation regarding the deck layout: no original deck plan seems to exist and we have our leading authority admitting that one deck plan would more or less do for the *Sir Lancelot*, the *Ariel* and the *Titania*!

Some of my readers will remember with pleasure the great days of the Model Engineer Exhibition during the immediate post-war years and will also recall with admiration the beautiful models of the *Sir Lancelot* and the *Ariel* exhibited so successfully by my old friend Ike Marsh of Barry Docks. These models were outstanding achievements by any yard-stick. It is through his kindness that I have a small batch of air letters originally sent to him by the Australian artist Mr D. M. Little. In these letters Little mentions other paintings he has done and they include various sketch plans and an interesting deck plan of the *Ariel* together with a most attractive colour scheme for the *Sir Lancelot* with pea-green boats, green bulwarks and green panels on the deckhouses, all of which I used on the larger of the two models.

53. *Carnarvon Castle* (1867)
Clipper

Waterline models, scales 32′ and 50′–1″, 9⅜″ and 6″ long respectively

One of Donald Currie's early Castle Line ships of a most handsome appearance with nicely raked masts and a long jibboom and flying jibboom. She also had somewhat unusual upside down painted ports, the white sill being shown above the black square and not below.

In the correspondence columns of the August 1936 issue of the old *Ships and Ship Models* there appeared a letter from a Mr John W. Juritz of Three Anchor Bay, South Africa, with a photo of a model of a very nice looking iron clipper, the *Carnarvon Castle*. Nearly twenty years later I wrote to Mr Juritz and in due course back came his data on the *Carnarvon Castle* from his relatives, he having died in the interval. One photo of the ship was available from the Nautical Photo Agency (all their negatives are now at Greenwich I believe) and Barclay, Curle & Co Ltd, the builders, very kindly let me have a photostat of the original hull lines which was all they had, it seemed. The personal and published help of the late Harold A. Underhill furnished further details, and the first of three models of the *Carnarvon Castle* was made.

The *Carnarvon Castle* model is a classic case of the 'abiding apprehension', mentioned in the introduction, coming home to roost. In 1968 the Cussons Collection of South African models was exhibited at the Cape Route Exhibition in London and one of the items supplied by the Union Castle Line was an excellent contemporary oil painting of the *Carnarvon Castle* which no one had seemed to know about when I enquired years before. This was photographed and fortunately showed the model to be remarkably correct. Since then many of the Clydeside firms have merged, and quantities of the old drawings have found their way to Greenwich. Among these is the deck and inboard profile drawing of the *Carnarvon Castle*!

One of the most useful books for this period is G. F. Campbell's *China Tea Clippers* published by Adlard Coles in 1954. The text is interesting and there are many detailed drawings, of Mr Campbell's usual high quality, of the various deck arrangements, fittings, equipment and rigging details of the clippers of the period.

The bow view picture of the *Carnarvon Castle* is of the smaller model at 50′–1″ and shows her under reduced canvas. The other model is under plain sail and flies the early Castle Line flag at the main and makes her number below the Red Ensign at the gaff peak.

54. *Thermopylae* (1868)
Clipper

Waterline model, scale 32′–1″, 9″ long

Designed by Bernard Waymouth and built by Walter Hood of Aberdeen for the famous Aberdeen White Star Line. She was composite built of rock elm and teak on iron frames, her tonnage was 948, length 212′, beam 36′ and depth 20′. Considered the *Cutty Sark*'s great rival and in Australia, at least, she was thought to be her superior.

A number of years ago when I did my first model of the *Thermopylae* I obtained, through the good offices of Ike Marsh, a set of blueprints of her by Mr H. N. Leask; the hull lines were those in Lubbock's *China Clippers* but where he got his deck plan and mast and spar dimensions from I have no idea.

David MacGregor in his *Fast Sailing Ships* gives us a completely new realization of the *Thermopylae*: a new set of lines from the offsets, a new sail plan from the original which had been languishing in the archives at Lloyd's Register, and a new deck plan, remarkably similar to Leask's I am glad to say.

However it is the deck plan which is of the most importance to the model builder and it is this item that is usually lacking in the detail one requires.

There are a few photos of the ship but nothing I know of giving such items as the number of panels and portholes in the deckhouse, the pin rail arrangement or the particular style of skylights. I have to say again that this is the kind of thing that is such an irritation to the serious ship model builder. One can draw a plan of a ship or paint a picture of a ship and get away with the minimum amount of information, but the ship model builder just has to know (or hope to know) more about the ship than anyone else.

55. *Cutty Sark* (1869)
Clipper

Waterline model, scale 32′–1″, 9⅛″ long

Like the frigate *Constitution* and Nelson's *Victory* the *Cutty Sark* is still with us; she is restored as nearly as may be to her pristine state at Greenwich so just for once there is no great difficulty regarding the research.

I am almost ashamed to say I have made seven models of this ship, the first so long ago that it had the misfortune to be bombed in the blitz on London. The first four were made largely from the Underhill drawings and the two volumes of *The Cutty Sark* by C. Nepean Longridge, whose large model, representing the ship in her Falmouth days, is at the Science Museum, South Kensington.

Dr Longridge must have been a remarkable man. He was, I believe, a ship's doctor and his two models, this *Cutty Sark* and the *Victory* already mentioned, are both superb pieces of craftsmanship.

The fifth model, illustrated here, was made after the ship herself was restored, after the discovery of the Tudgay painting and after the publication of Mr G. F. Campbell's magnificent set of plans. It was presented by my client to HRH the Duke of Edinburgh in 1963.

About the middle of 1968 I decided to do, on my own account, a sixth model for exhibition in London during 1969 by way of my own modest little celebration of the ship's centenary, but this model got itself sold before the centennial year even commenced. Not to be beaten, the seventh (and I am bound to say the final) model was commenced over the turn of that year for the same purpose, but this too, like the proverbial hot cakes, went at the beginning of 1969. As a matter

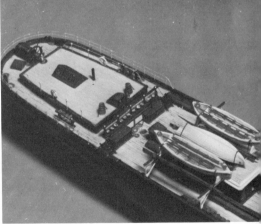

of interest the fifth and sixth models have cases of bird's-eye maple, and pre-stained samples of this veneer were taken up to Greenwich and matched with the bird's-eye maple panelling in the captain's cabin on the ship so that the two cases correspond well with the original. One of the two centennial models shows the ship with bare yards at anchor in calm conditions and the other in rougher weather with reefs taken in her fore course and main upper topsail.

56. *Servia* (1881)
Cunard liner

Waterline model, scale 50′–1″, 10¾″ long (colour plate p. 110)

Built by J. & G. Thomson Ltd at Clydebank, the *Servia* was the first merchant ship to be built entirely of Siemen's mild steel. She had an overall length of 544′ and a beam of 52′ and was apparently the first Cunarder to be provided with electric light. She was rigged as a three-masted barque with Cunningham's Patent self-reefing gear on the fore and main topsail yards.

She was a handsome vessel with an elegant profile and a remarkably compli-cated and fragile looking three-decker navigation bridge.

The *Servia* displays a particular feature of ships of this period, that of the skid skylight. Fitted along the base of the deckhouses by a clever arrangement it affords light and air to the inboard cabins and alley ways below.

I was able to obtain only three photos of the actual ship, one of which showed the hull plating very clearly, including the slightly unusual external butt straps along the depth of two strakes amidships. It is very rare indeed to be able to get a shell plating expansion among the ship's drawings and almost always the arrangement of hull plating has to be taken from photographs.

As well as the three photos the research was nicely taken care of by Harold A. Underhill's plans, comprising hull lines (which he was honest enough to say were 'not authoritative' but work out very well in practice), general arrange-ment and masts, spars and rigging.

There is also the large and detailed model in the Science Museum. This is a typical example of Victorian model building, not at all realistic, with the usual plated and polished metal work about the decks and a high-gloss, unplated hull, but nevertheless full of useful detail which can be rendered in a realistic fashion on a realistic waterline model.

I am always more than pleased when there is one of these large models of a ship that I wish to build still in existence, especially when I am allowed to take colour photos of it as I was in this instance.

There are some minor differences between the Science Museum model and the Underhill plans which could not be resolved by the photographs of the ship, but they were very minor indeed.

The model shows the ship under power with all her sails furled. She flies the red and gold, lion and globe Cunard flag and was apparently the first new Cunard ship to do so.

57. USS *Oregon* (1895)
US warship

Waterline model, scale 32′–1″, 11″ long

This model produced a unique situation where the American client knew a great deal more about the ship than did the model builder.

He had been doing research on this particular ship for years before he came to me to have a model built, and consequently showered me with large rolls of plans, many black and white photos of the *Oregon* and her sisters, plus a set of stereo colour slides of the very large-scale model of the vessel in the Bremerton Navy Yard, Washington.

By modern standards the *Oregon* was quite a small vessel, about 350′ long, but like most warships of the period had an immense amount of detail, especially in the central structure, a good deal of which is not easily seen as it occurs below the boats and the bridge connecting the two funnels.

Difficult though these items certainly are to see, the space left by their omission would show glaringly, I am sure.

The *Oregon* model is an excellent example of how important it is to ensure the correct sequence of fitting and assembly in doing a detailed model.

The ship's boats proved most interesting, as I had many official large-scale drawings of them, and they were quite different from Royal Navy boats of the period. During her life the *Oregon* had been altered a number of times and appeared in different colour schemes. The model shows her in her heyday with a dark red boottopping, a white hull and all her superstructure a very warm buff colour. The barrels of the large guns are grey, the small ones black, her boats white with black rubbing strakes and the inside of her vent cowls red. A very attractive vessel.

The ship is shown at anchor in a calm sea, the stern awning spread, the others furled, the port whaleboat, with sails spilling, is at the gangway, another boat is in the offing and her steam cutter at the starboard boom.

5 THE TWENTIETH CENTURY

58. *Herzogin Cecilie* (1902)
Four-masted barque

Waterline model, scale 32′–1″, 11⅝″ long

This is the second model of this ship I have made. The first was from the drawings by Mr Edward Bowness, appearing as supplements in the 1937 and 1938 *Ships and Ship Models*, and these plans were used again together with those of Harold A. Underhill, and the builder's plans reproduced in W. L. A. Derby's *The Tall Ships Pass*.

She was a greatly photographed ship and many photos are available, but unfortunately not very many show her in her original state. However the model depicts her in her early days before the carved trail boards were removed and various other alterations occurred.

On these latter day square-riggers there is a great deal of interesting deck detail to do. This is carefully shown on the plans and most of it is confirmable from the numerous photos taken on board. The rigging, however, is a trifle monotonous as there are three virtually identical masts.

The *Herzogin Cecilie* is depicted at anchor with all her sails furled, and shows the rather curious method of stowing the staysails in vogue at this time. I am always at a loss to know how such a large area of canvas can be furled into a neat, tapering curved tube. It is just not possible to do it with a whole, scale-sized staysail on the model, which shows I suppose that the material used does not 'compress' to scale.

The *Herzogin Cecilie* was built by the Bremerhaven firm of Rickmers for use as a cargo-cadet ship for the North German Lloyd line. Her length between perpendiculars was 308′ 2″ and she had a beam over the frames of 46′. She was interned in Chile during the 1914–18 war and was subsequently French owned until 1922, when she was sold to her most famous owner, Gustaf Erikson, who ran her until 1936 when, in April of that year, she went on the rocks near Salcombe during a thick fog.

Salvage was attempted and some of her gear removed but nearly three years after stranding she suddenly capsized during a gale and disappeared.

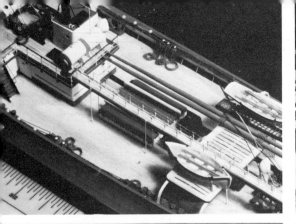

59. *Armadale Castle* (1903)
Union Castle liner

Waterline model, scale 32′–1″, 18⅜″ long (colour plate p. 111)

The *Armadale Castle* was built by the Fairfield Shipbuilding & Engineering Co Ltd of Glasgow. She had a gross tonnage of 12,973, moulded dimensions of 570′ 0″ × 64′ 3″ × 42′ 6″ and a load waterline length of 569′ 0″. Twin-screw quadruple expansion engines gave her a speed of 16 to 17 knots.

The *Armadale* and her sister the *Kenilworth Castle* were the first mail steamers ordered after the amalgamation of the Union and Castle Lines, and replaced the Union liner *Scot* and the Castle liner *Dunvegan Castle*.

The vessel was named after a property in the Isle of Skye owned by the MacDonalds and she was launched by Lady MacDonald of the Isles.

Her first commander was Captain J. C. Robinson and on her third voyage to the Cape she became the first mail steamer to cross the Durban bar and berth in the inner dock. Most of her life was spent on the Cape mail service, but during World War I she was fitted with 4·7″ guns and served as an armed merchant cruiser attached to the Cape Station. During the campaign against German South-West Africa she was frequently in action and bombarded and destroyed the wireless station at Swakopmund and later Cape Cross.

After the war she resumed her normal activities as a very popular passenger liner on the Cape route, being finally sold for scrap in 1936.

The *Armadale Castle* was a typical tropical waters vessel of her day with open shade decks and well over a hundred ventilators and some forty-four skylights cluttering up her deck spaces. Her very tall (53′ 6″) funnels perhaps seem too obtrusive to modern eyes, but they have their own grace and proportion and with the pleasant and distinctive Union Castle colour scheme make for a vessel of very satisfactory appearance.

The model was made from the builder's original hand-drawn draughts, which were done at a scale of 4′–1″, and so comprehensive that I produced one of the most detailed models I have done.

Large photographs were obtained of the builder's shipyard model, and most interesting and perhaps most useful of all were some twenty photographs of the actual ship at various periods during her career. These showed quite a number of small alterations carried out on the ship from time to time, mainly on the bridge, the boat davits and W/T accommodation. The model shows the ship in her original condition as designed.

The magnificent plans mentioned above and the large photographs were all borrowed through the good offices of the owners. Small sample tins of the actual paint used on the Union Castle ships were also obtained, and whilst this paint was too coarse and shiny to use on the model, matching shades of suitable paint were mixed and used. The lavender grey of the Union Castle hulls is especially difficult to match.

The *Armadale Castle* appears here tide rode, moored to a single buoy by a slip rope. An awning is spread over the poop deck, the cargo hatches are boarded but

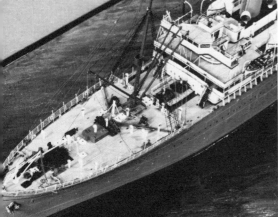

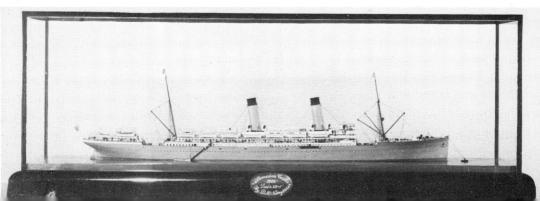

not yet canvas covered, the derricks are shown raised and completely rigged with whips and guys still bent. The lifeboats are all covered, the poop whalers open, the port gig hangs from the davits in the outboard position, and the starboard gig is still tied to the after starboard accommodation ladder.

The usual Red Ensign flies from the stern and the new amalgamated Union Castle house flag flies at the main truck. The Blue Peter at the foremast together with the slip rope indicate an immediate departure.

60. *Waratah* (1908)
Blue Anchor liner

Waterline model, scale 32′–1″, 15⅜″ long

The *Waratah* was built by Barclay Curle of Whiteinch, Glasgow, for Lund's Blue Anchor Line. She was a twin-screwed vessel intended for the Australia run, and was named after *Telopea speciosissima*, commonly known as the New South Wales waratah, the state flower.

On the return half of her maiden voyage from Australia to Britain she docked at Durban. Having re-coaled there she left the dockside, with 92 passengers and 119 crew, on the evening of 26 July 1909 in perfect weather conditions. At 6 o'clock the next morning she exchanged signals with the *Clan MacIntyre*, doing a steady 13 knots and in perfect trim.

This was the last ever seen of the *Waratah*. She had no radio, she left no wreckage, no survivors, no trace at all.

Just what did happen to her has been the cause of much conjecture ever since, the most usual theory is that she was top-heavy and capsized in a gale, because apparently she was built one deck higher than any of Lund's previous vessels, but an inspection of the builder's plans and indeed a look at the model makes this appear unlikely.

Another, perhaps more credible, theory is that although she was late leaving Durban she left before her coal was properly stowed in the bunkers, and it is possible that this was left piled on the decks to such an extent as to affect her stability in adverse weather.

The usual Court of Enquiry was held but could hardly be expected to reach any useful conclusions. The following year the owners went out of business and sold their remaining vessels to the P & O Line.

It is well known that shipbuilders are most unwilling to supply the least information about the ships they have built and which they consider unsuccessful or unlucky. At the time this model was first suggested I had a friend at court in Whiteinch, and although he went as high as possible no plans were forthcoming. Some three years later after a good deal of trouble and via a very circuitous route my client managed to obtain copies of the detailed, general arrangement drawings. On an occasion some time previous to this the same kind of brickwall was encountered regarding drawings for a model of the *Titanic*, although the situation regarding this ship has eased a little recently.

Only a few photos taken of the ship during her very short life were found,

and considerable further research was undertaken to try and discover if the builder's model still existed, and also to try and find further photographs – but without result. I feel sure there must have been a builder's model and that it is still around somewhere.

The Blue Anchor colour scheme was obtained from Mr J. Wilhelm of New Orleans, an expert on steam vessels of this period. She had a black hull, red boottopping and coffee-coloured upper works. Her masts and most of her ventilators were brown. The latter were blue inside the cowls and it is, of course, a blue anchor on the white band of the funnel.

The first-class smoke room on the after part of the boat deck has an open alcove facing the stern. This is equipped with bench seats and tables. There is much the same arrangement on the deck immediately below and the white tablecloths can be seen in the illustrations.

One of the notable features of the old-fashioned tropical ship were the awning stanchions and frames. There are a great many of these and they are very precisely involved with much else on the ship (the derricks, rigging, etc) and are especially difficult to fit.

The *Waratah* is depicted commencing her maiden voyage and meeting, off her port bow, the staysail rigged Thames sailing barge *Dreadnought*, built at Sittingbourne in 1907 and still working when the model was made.

61. HM Warships (c World War II)
(*Warspite, Cottesmore, Ulysses* and *Cassandra*)

Waterline models, scale 100′–1″, $6\frac{3}{8}''$, $3\frac{1}{2}''$, $3\frac{1}{2}''$ and $2\frac{3}{4}''$ long

Norman Ough was the great exponent of modern warship modelling and fortunately has left us a number of excellent plans of the period, but even he could not get all the information he needed. In 1961 when these models were built it was still a difficult period in this respect (far different from today when there seems to be a plethora of warship plans commercially available) and these models were mostly made from the details obtained from a mass of photographs, *Jane's Fighting Ships* and some rather sketchy Admiralty model plans.

At 100′–1″ these are the smallest scaled models in the book and generally speaking such small-scale models are rarely, if ever, rigged or fitted with deck rails. These ones are, and there is no reason why this should not always be done as remarkably fine wire is available, suitable for the rigging and deck rails, and other small details offer no particular problem.

Indeed in the light of subsequent work I believe there is no reason why deck and hull planking and hull plating should not be done at 1/1200″, although it was not done on these models.

The great thing with very-small-scale models is to get out of one's head the convention that just because it is small this is an excuse to do only half a job. I remember before the war doing a great many 100′–1″ waterline models, each no

better than the last. This too, still seems to be a practice among workers at this scale. Quantity and uniformity seem to be the order of the day and this is a pity as there is a lot more to be done at 100′–1″ and if the general viewer has to use a magnifying glass then why not?

62. *Rhodesia Castle* (1951)
Union Castle liner

Waterline model, scale 16′–1″, 36″ long

Built by Harland and Wolff at Belfast and launched on 5 April 1951, the *Rhodesia Castle* had an overall length of 576′ and a gross tonnage of 17,041. She was a one-class ship designed to carry 530 passengers on the Union Castle round-Africa service.

The model was something of an innovation. It was the first 16′–1″ model I had done, the first model I made deliberately to sell and, although it was not a commission, it did have a price ceiling. So on the principle of overcoming all the difficulties at one go, at the outset it was an excellent subject!

Although it was for use in a shipping office window I was quite determined not to do the usual glossy hull and plated fittings, etc and intended to finish the model in my normal realistic way with non-shiny planked decks, hull plated to scale with punched ports and windows and with matt or semi-matt paint.

The owners obtained the complete set of builder's plans and a number of photographs so I had pretty well everything I needed. Nevertheless I remember it as being a somewhat 'anxious' model to build, perhaps caused by lack of professional experience and the jump from 50′–1″ to 16′–1″. However when completed the model was well received and accepted.

Its exhibition in the company's Fenchurch Street windows caused much interest and occasioned an article in the *Journal of Commerce* and I think it may well have been the first realistic shipping office window model.

The *Rhodesia Castle* herself is now under a foreign flag I believe and this model was accidentally dropped and badly damaged. I am not sure of its subsequent fate.

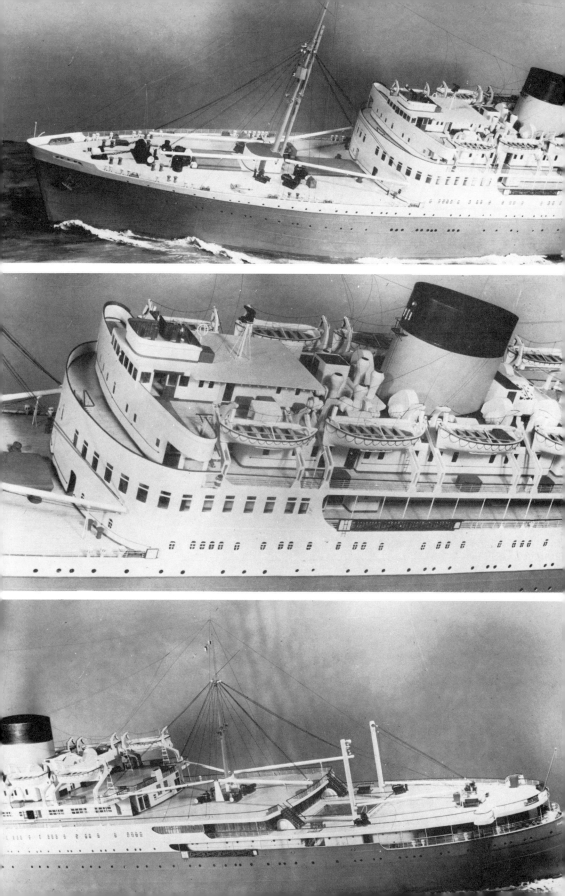

63. HMY *Britannia* (1953)
Royal yacht

Waterline model, scale 32′–1″, 13″ long (colour plate p. 111)

The first model of the *Britannia* I made was to a smaller scale than this example and was done quite soon after she came out.

I had the builder's original plans, a quantity of tracings I took in the DNC's Department at the Admiralty and an excellent set of photographs by the late Edward Bowness, but try as we would my wife and I could not get on board to make notes and take our own photographs.

Some fifteen years later I decided to do a further model at a larger scale, and on this occasion we did manage to board her, armed with stereo and ½-frame cameras and tape recorder.

During the interval quite a few, somewhat confusing, alterations had been carried out on the ship and she was at the time of our visit about due for another major refit and overhaul with further alterations to be done, so this second model also shows her in her original 1953 appearance.

The famous photographers, Bekens of Cowes, Isle of Wight, who have a vast collection of ship photographs going back a surprisingly long way, supplied some large photographs of the Royal Yacht taken during various Cowes Weeks, showing her moored to a buoy and dressed overall, and she is shown like this here.

The Royal Barge, with its Royal Standard struck in the bows, is in the water at the after starboard accommodation ladder and one of the launches is at the port boom. The Royal racing yacht, the Flying Fifteen *Coweslip*, is off the port bow.

I am quite sure the exact order of dressing flags for Her Majesty's ships is all neatly laid down in some Royal Navy signal manual, but the only Navy publication I happen to have is a 1943 *Seaman's Pocket Book* where it does not appear, so the best part of a morning's work went on plotting out the order from stem to stern from the various photographs. Signal flags are intended to be read from their design alone so the fact that they were black and white photographs didn't matter. However the winds, at the moments of exposure, were not entirely favourable and one or two flags remained obscure, but by dredging the archives and getting out the newspaper cuttings of King George V's Jubilee Review at Spithead, which I had carefully saved at the time, I found that the order of flags was much the same then as now and the remaining few difficulties were overcome. I think the order of flags is quite correct.

Quite by chance the day we visited the *Britannia* was a very curious flag flying day indeed, as it happened to be the anniversary of the Queen's Coronation and at the same time one of the nine days of court mourning for the death of HRH the Duke of Windsor. Consequently we had a Rear Admiral's flag at the fore and white ensigns at the main and mizzen, all at the truck, with the Union Jack at the bow and the white ensign at the stern both at half mast on their staffs. Had it not been for the above sad circumstance she would have been dressed overall.

The hull of the *Britannia* is of flush plating and finished with a remarkable high-gloss blue paint and in the usual way I obtained some samples of her actual paint and matched them with paint of a suitable texture and finish for the model.

These rare ships with such brilliant paintwork pose a problem for the model builder as one cannot have a full-sized gloss on the model. The amount of shine has to be scaled down and on dark colours like the *Britannia*'s blue the judicious rubbing down to reduce the gloss appears to lighten the shade and it is a matter of some precision gently to re-polish the hull to regain the dark tone without the excessive gloss.

64. *Sir Winston Churchill* (c1969)
Training schooner

Waterline model, scale 16′–1″, 10¼″ long (colour plate p. 108)

Designed by Camper & Nicholson of Southampton and built by Richard Dunston Ltd of Hessle, Yorkshire in 1966 for the Sail Training Association.

Her dimensions were: length overall 134·75′, length on the waterline 103·167′ breadth moulded 24·96′. A most interesting subject for a model and at the time of her building quite unlike any other sailing vessel.

The acquisition of data for this model started off in a very low key with a number of sheets of the original design, which of course had been subject to many alterations. This situation was soon changed when a complete set of the builder's lines and general arrangement drawings came to hand, and during the course of building many sheets of her fittings, masts, boats, etc also arrived.

Bekens of Cowes had available some of their large photos of the *Sir Winston* under sail, and I obtained two mast, sail and rigging drawings in colour, one by A. Challis and the other by C. V. Waine. And finally my client supplied some three dozen colour slides all of close-ups taken on board.

The result of all these data is of course a very detailed model, and although this amount of work takes a long time to do, one has the satisfaction of knowing that virtually nothing has been left out.

65. *Bloodhound* (c1969)
Royal racing yacht

Waterline model, scale 6'–1", 10½" long

It could be said that the scale of this model makes it too large for inclusion in a book of miniatures, but this was the smallest scale I was allowed and as the model is for a special purpose it may be thought appropriate to end this book with it.

The model was commissioned with something under a three-month deadline, from cold to completion. A tall order with no research done and I frankly admit little knowledge of modern yachts. If it had been one of Charles II's yachts of 300 years earlier there would have been hardly any problem.

However, a somewhat similar situation arose to that of the previous model, and I was greatly helped by many people most notably by Mr John B. Wood of Camper & Nicholson, an expert and enthusiastic photographer who supplied me with quantities of black and white and colour pictures taken when the yacht was moored at Gosport. Indeed without his help I could not have done the model at all. As ever, Bekens yielded their usual excellent 'at sea' pictures.

The drawings produced something of a problem, garnered as they were from various naval architects and yacht builders who, at one time or another, had been concerned with several alterations and modifications carried out on the vessel. So apart from the hull lines and the basic dimensions of fittings etc, great reliance was placed on the photographs and on many helpful discussions with people specifically connected with her recent racing activities.

The *Bloodhound*'s hull is even shinier than the *Britannia*'s but a slightly different shade of blue, and as this was rather a large-scale model I used the actual 'full-sized' paint. I don't recall before having to lay deckplanks curved to the deckline shape of the hull, but they are like this on the *Bloodhound* and are nibbed into an extra wide, varnished plank down the centreline. My photographic expert had taken the trouble to have himself hauled up to the masthead, and had photographed the entire deck from there so just for once I was able to get the correct number of planks with all their butts properly arranged. Two complete decks were produced before a reasonable result was obtained.

As a pre-war model builder properly brought up, as it were, on the precepts of the late Lt Cmdr J. H. Craine, RNR (Jason) I cannot help wondering what he would think of the brilliant red, blue and green synthetic ropes of the *Bloodhound*, in view of his frequent strictures on the conventional rigging of ships to keep the ropes on the model dark, thin and unobtrusive.

To an eye versed in the simplicities of old-fashioned square rig there are some very strange sheet arrangements on the *Bloodhound*, but I am assured on the best authority they are correct, and I see they are for myself from the Beken photos, but it all looks unreasonably complicated.

This model of the *Bloodhound* was presented to HRH the Duke of Edinburgh by the Royal Yachting Association during the meeting of their council on board HMY *Britannia* on 5 August 1970. The presentation marked the completion of fourteen years during which Prince Philip had served as President of the Royal Yachting Association.

GLOSSARY

The models in the foregoing pages cover some 2,600 years and in referring to this very brief glossary it should perhaps be borne in mind that the meanings of some technical words and phrases changed over that period.

Aback	Said of square sails when they are so trimmed as to take the wind on their forward surfaces in order to take the way off the ship
Aportlast	Of lower yards, when still athwartship – they are lowered to their fullest extent to help the stability of a vessel in heavy weather
Apostis	The outriggers to take the oars of a galley
Bed	The base of a gun carriage secured to the rear axle and upon which in turn the quoin rests
Bomb	An abbreviation for 'bomb-ketch' or 'bomb-vessel'. Generally a two-masted craft with reinforced deck to take a large mortar or howitzer
Bonnet	The removable, bottom section of a lower square sail, much in use before the introduction of reefing
Bunt	The middle portion of a square sail controlled by bunt lines, hence the expression, of sails partly hauled up 'hanging in their bunts'
Carronade	A gun of shorter barrel, lighter weight, larger bore, shorter range and requiring less crew than the usual cannon and more often mounted on slides than on carriages
Cheeks	The sides or main upright pieces of a gun carriage
Crane–line	A simple halyard from mast top to deck especially in the days of the carracks used to take missiles up to the top-men
Crowsfoot	A fan–like arrangement of rope intended to spread the pull of the main rope to which it is attached
Demi–cannon	Smaller than a 'normal' cannon, there were ordinary demi-cannon and extraordinary demi–cannon all varying in length of barrel and weight of shot, the specifications also varying from one period to another
Embolon	The ram of a galley
Fancy rail	One of the rails and mouldings along the length of a ship. A name particularly associated with American clipper ships and usually the uppermost or topgallant rail on these vessels
Frames	The 'ribs' of a ship's hull, also called timbers
Futtock ends	The butts of the various double sections of timber comprising a hull frame
Girdled	An extra layer of planking put on a ship's hull about the waterline to increase beam and stability
Hanging knees	Brackets generally connecting deckbeams to hull timbers, latterly of iron but when of wood ideally with the grain of the

175

	wood following the curve made by the two arms. Lodge knees were fitted horizontally, hanging knees vertically downwards, standard knees vertically upwards and dagger knees diagonally
Jolly-watt	From a contemporary document refers specifically to the smallest of the 'Prince Royal's' boats and probably the equivalent of the more modern jolly boat
Lateen	A triangular fore-&-aft sail bent to a yard; frequently on the after masts of northern vessels but of more versatile use in southern waters
Leeches	The side edges of square sails and the after edge of fore and aft sails
Martnets	Complicated crowsfeet attached to the leeches of sails and used in furling. Superseded by simple leech lines and brails
Parrel	An assemblage of wooden ribs and revolving wooden balls encircling a mast and attached with rope to the centre of a yard, allowing the latter to travel up and down the mast as required
Pavise	The part of the rail on early vessels hung with pavises or curved shields
Poke	The bag on a crane-line for carrying ammunition
Quoin	The wedge shaped wooden block in a gun carriage used to elevate or depress the muzzle of the gun
Ringtail	A gaff sail's fore and aft stuns'l, or extension. Usually bent to a small yard hoisted to the peak of the gaff
Sakers	Smaller carriage guns with the usual classification of ordinary and extraordinary, plus that of 'lite' sakers and the ultimate refinement of 'sakers of the least size'
Square tuck	The lower part of the stern built flat with diagonal planking either side of the stern post, as opposed to the round tuck formed by running the hull planking in a smooth sweep round and up to the transom. Square tucked vessels were known as 'butter box arsed'
Stopper and shank painter	An arrangement of ropes securing an anchor in such a way as to let it go on the instant should the need arise
Tampions	Wooden plugs inserted in the muzzles of guns to keep out the sea water
Tide-rode	Said of a ship riding to a single anchor or moored to a single buoy when she points between wind and tide but influenced more by the latter
Trucks	The wooden wheels of gun carriages
Trunnions	Projecting stubs on the sides of cannon to support them on the cheeks of the carriage in such a way as to allow the elevation or depression of the barrel